DEFENSE, SECURITY AND STRATEGIES

NATIONAL BIOSURVEILLANCE STRATEGY AND ASSOCIATED SCIENCE AND TECHNOLOGY ROADMAPS

CONSIDERATIONS AND PRIORITIES

DEFENSE, SECURITY AND STRATEGIES

Additional books in this series can be found on Nova's website under the Series tab.

Additional e-books in this series can be found on Nova's website under the e-book tab.

DEFENSE, SECURITY AND STRATEGIES

NATIONAL BIOSURVEILLANCE STRATEGY AND ASSOCIATED SCIENCE AND TECHNOLOGY ROADMAPS

CONSIDERATIONS AND PRIORITIES

AMANDA WENDELL
EDITOR

NOVINKA

New York

For permission to use material from this book please contact us:
Telephone 631-231-7269; Fax 631-231-8175
Web Site: http://www.novapublishers.com

Additional color graphics may be available in the e-book version of this book.

LIBRARY OF CONGRESS CATALOGING-IN-PUBLICATION DATA

ISBN: 978-1-62948-994-0

Published by Nova Science Publishers, Inc. † New York

CONTENTS

PREFACE

A well-integrated, national biosurveillance enterprise is a national security imperative. The United States' ability to detect quickly and characterize a potential incident of national significance that affects human, animal, or plant health is of paramount importance. Rapid detection and enhanced situational awareness are critical to saving lives and improving incident outcomes, whether the result of a bioterrorism attack or other weapons of mass destruction (WMD) threat, an emerging infectious disease, pandemic, environmental disaster, or a food-borne illness. Beyond the need to protect domestic interests, and because health threats transcend national borders, the United States also plays a vital role within an international network of biosurveillance centers across the globe. This book focuses on the national strategy for biosurveillance and the national biosurveillance science and technology roadmap.

Chapter 1 - A well-integrated, national biosurveillance enterprise is a national security imperative. Our ability to detect quickly and characterize a potential incident of national significance that affects human, animal, or plant health is of paramount importance. Rapid detection and enhanced situational awareness are critical to saving lives and improving incident outcomes, whether the result of a bioterror attack or other weapons of mass destruction (WMD) threat, an emerging infectious disease, pandemic, environmental disaster, or a food-borne illness. Beyond our need to protect domestic interests, and because health threats transcend national borders, the United States also plays a vital role within an international network of biosurveillance centers across the globe. For years, there have been dedicated efforts to promote and strengthen biosurveillance capabilities. There exists a strong foundation of capacity arrayed in a tiered architecture of Federal, State, local, tribal, territorial, and private capabilities. We can strengthen the approach with focused attention on a few core functions and an increased integration of effort across the Nation. In these fiscally challenging times, we seek to leverage distributed capabilities and to add value to independent, individual efforts to protect the health and safety of the Nation through an effective national biosurveillance enterprise.

A key to improving all-hazards incident management is to focus efforts on collecting, analyzing, and disseminating information to facilitate timely decisionmaking, whether a health incident is a naturally occurring phenomenon, accidental, or deliberate in nature. From the individual, to primary care providers, to hospital practitioners, to state and local health officers, to Federal entities responsible for health emergency response, to the President of the United States, there exists an imperative to identify incidents early and to make decisions swiftly to save lives, even amidst great uncertainty. The goal is to achieve *a well-integrated national biosurveillance enterprise that saves lives by providing essential information for better decisionmaking at all levels.* Our Strategy is to integrate and enhance national biosurveillance efforts to answer specific key questions that guide decisionmaking in times of crisis; enable more rapid detection and foster improved situational awareness by further extending a dynamic, distributed national network of expertise and capabilities; and put into practice new thinking to facilitate decisionmaking processes in conditions of significant ambiguity. This enhanced national biosurveillance capability will be applied broadly to identify and understand potential human, animal, or plant health impacts resulting from chemical, biological, radiological, and nuclear (CBRN) and environmental incidents, as well as influenza and other public health trends, all of which may also be leveraged in the service of global health efforts.

We must be resolved to strengthen life-saving biosurveillance capabilities within our existing resources. We can do this by leveraging more effectively our existing national network of expertise and capabilities, and through targeted enhancements that provide benefits across the enterprise. There are no higher priorities than the health, well being, and security of the American people.

Chapter 2 - The *National Strategy for Biosurveillance* (*Strategy*), published in July 2012, calls for "a coordinated approach that brings together Federal, state, local, and tribal governments; the private sector; nongovernmental organizations; and international partners" to enhance existing biosurveillance capabilities and, where necessary, develop new ones that provide decision makers and responders with the essential information they need to mitigate impacts of threats to health and associated economic, societal, and political consequences. The *Strategy* recognizes that a well-integrated national biosurveillance enterprise can saves lives by providing essential information for better decision making at all levels.

The interagency Biosurveillance Science and Technology Working Group (BST WG), chartered in May 2012, was established under the Subcommittee on Biological Defense Research and Development of the National Science and Technology Council's Committee on Homeland and National Security to develop national biosurveillance research and development priorities to enable the Core Functions of the *Strategy*.

Chapter 3 - A catastrophic biological incident could threaten the Nation's human, animal, plant, environmental, and economic health, as well as America's national security. Such an event would demand a quick and effective response in order to minimize loss of life and other adverse consequences and, in the case of suspected criminal activity or terrorism, to thwart ongoing activity and prevent follow-on attacks. But response and recovery from a catastrophic biological incident is not a simple, formulaic process. Rather, it is a continuous process of data and information collection, evidence-based review, and decision making, all leading to an informed and constantly evolving series of critical and coordinated actions. Moreover, the response and recovery process involves the integration and coordination of data and capabilities from many different sectors, including public health, law enforcement, waste management, infrastructure management, and transportation. Strategic science and technology (S&T) investments are essential to provide the information that can support evidence-based operational decisions and strengthen response-and-recovery efforts. *This report categorizes key scientific knowledge gaps, identifies technology solutions to these gaps, and prioritizes research areas that will enable government at all levels to make decisions more effectively during the response to, and recovery from, biological incidents.*

The prioritized, near-term objectives and broader, long-term goals presented in this report constitute a roadmap for use by Federal departments and agencies to coordinate their research and development (R&D) activities. The primary near-term objectives whose timely achievement this roadmap aims to facilitate are:

- Establish the location(s) of the confirmed biological agent in the environment;

- Develop reliable estimates of risk of exposure for a multitude of environments, matrices, and conditions associated with wide-area release scenarios;
- Develop reliable estimates of risk to humans, animals, and plants through various exposure and transmission routes;
- Develop risk reduction strategies, including decontamination, waste management, contaminant control, and reaerosolization control, for a variety of biological threats and scenarios;
- Evaluate population infection prevention measures (e.g., quarantine, isolation, and social distancing) used to reduce incident impact and develop a strong scientific basis for recommending these measures; and
- Use risk communication research to guide development of appropriate messages and dissemination means to stakeholders, including decision makers, first responders, the public, and the media.

Coordination of R&D agendas among Federal departments and agencies will reduce duplication of effort and enhance efficiencies as the Nation enhances its capacity to prevent, protect against, mitigate, respond to, and recover from catastrophic biological incidents.

In: National Biosurveillance Strategy ... ISBN: 978-1-62948-994-0
Editor: Amanda Wendell

Chapter 1

NATIONAL STRATEGY FOR BIOSURVEILLANCE*

Executive Office of the President

THE WHITE HOUSE

July 31, 2012

There is no higher priority than the security and safety of the American people. As a Nation, we must be prepared for the full range of threats, including a terrorist attack involving a biological agent, the spread of infectious diseases, and food-borne illnesses. The effective dissemination of a lethal biological agent, for instance, could endanger the lives of hundreds of thousands of people and result in untold economic, societal, and political consequences.

In my *National Security Strategy*, I committed the United States to new approaches to counter biological threats. Specifically, I called for "obtaining timely and accurate insight on current and emerging risks." Such biosurveillance -- including early detection -- is one of our first lines of defense against these threats. As we saw during the H1N1 influenza pandemic of 2009, decisionmakers -- from the President to local officials -- need accurate and timely information in order to develop the effective responses

* This document was released by the Executive Office of the President, July 2012.

that save lives. The sooner we can detect and understand a threat, the faster we can take action to protect the American people.

This first-ever *National Strategy for Biosurveillance* builds on the capabilities already in place and further institutionalizes our efforts to ensure that we are doing everything possible to identify and understand threats as early as possible. Its goal is to provide the critical information and ongoing situational awareness that enables better decisionmaking at all levels. It calls for a coordinated approach that brings together Federal, State, local, and tribal governments; the private sector; nongovernmental organizations; and international partners.

It challenges us to take full advantage of the advanced technologies, new vaccines, the latest science, and social media that can help keep our citizens safe. It describes the core functions and critical capabilities we need to succeed.

As a next step, I am directing that a strategic implementation plan be completed within 120 days to lay out the specific actions that are required and the responsibilities of all partners in this mission. In the event of a biological outbreak or incident, the threat will move rapidly and transcend boundaries and borders. So must our response. Guided by this *Strategy*, I am confident that we can meet our shared responsibility and deepen the collaboration we need to keep our country safe and secure.

INTRODUCTION

A well-integrated, national biosurveillance enterprise is a national security imperative. Our ability to detect quickly and characterize a potential incident of national significance that affects human, animal, or plant health is of paramount importance. Rapid detection and enhanced situational awareness are critical to saving lives and improving incident outcomes, whether the result of a bioterror attack or other weapons of mass destruction (WMD) threat, an emerging infectious disease, pandemic, environmental disaster, or a food-borne illness. Beyond our need to protect domestic interests, and because health threats transcend national borders, the United States also plays a vital role within an international network of biosurveillance centers across the globe. For years, there have been dedicated efforts to promote and strengthen biosurveillance capabilities. There exists a strong foundation of capacity arrayed in a tiered architecture of Federal, State, local, tribal, territorial, and private capabilities. We can strengthen the approach with focused attention on a few core functions and an increased integration of effort across the Nation. In these fiscally challenging times, we seek to leverage distributed capabilities and to add value to independent, individual efforts to protect the health and safety of the Nation through an effective national biosurveillance enterprise.

A key to improving all-hazards incident management is to focus efforts on collecting, analyzing, and disseminating information to facilitate timely decisionmaking, whether a health incident is a naturally occurring phenomenon, accidental, or deliberate in nature. From the individual, to primary care providers, to hospital practitioners, to state and local health officers, to Federal entities responsible for health emergency response, to the President of the United States, there exists an imperative to identify incidents early and to make decisions swiftly to save lives, even amidst great uncertainty. The goal is to achieve *a well-integrated national biosurveillance enterprise that saves lives by providing essential information for better decisionmaking at all levels.* Our Strategy is to integrate and enhance national biosurveillance efforts to answer specific key questions that guide decisionmaking in times of crisis; enable more rapid detection and foster improved situational awareness by further extending a dynamic, distributed national network of expertise and capabilities; and put into practice new thinking to facilitate decisionmaking processes in conditions of significant ambiguity. This enhanced national biosurveillance capability will be applied broadly to identify and understand potential human, animal, or plant health impacts resulting from chemical, biological, radiological, and nuclear (CBRN) and environmental incidents, as well as influenza and other public health trends, all of which may also be leveraged in the service of global health efforts.

We must be resolved to strengthen life-saving biosurveillance capabilities within our existing resources. We can do this by leveraging more effectively our existing national network of expertise and capabilities, and through targeted enhancements that provide benefits across the enterprise. There are no higher priorities than the health, well being, and security of the American people.

Overview of the National Strategy for Biosurveillance

The *National Strategy for Biosurveillance* sets forth the United States Government approach to strengthen our national biosurveillance enterprise and describes a core set of functions critical to this Strategy's success. The approach builds on existing biosurveillance concepts and capabilities in seeking to enable more rapid detection, knowledge, and characterization of human, animal, or plant disease activity to enhance incident situational awareness. At the same time, this Strategy outlines an approach that is more selective and deliberate in its intent.

The Strategy defines biosurveillance as the process of gathering, integrating, interpreting, and communicating essential information related to all-hazards threats or disease activity affecting human, animal, or plant health to achieve early detection and warning, contribute to overall situational awareness of the health aspects of an incident, and to enable better decisionmaking at all levels. This definition is consistent with that of Homeland Security Presidential Directive-21 and now emphasizes an all-hazards scope and informed decisionmaking.'

This *National Biosurveillance Strategy* flows from the *National Security Strategy*, which highlights the importance of disease surveillance for public health threats, and is consistent with the *National Strategy for Countering Biological Threats*, which emphasizes information sharing among Federal departments and agencies to identify biological threats.

The Federal Government seeks to galvanize action across the Nation to further extend and integrate our distributed national biosurveillance enterprise. Where efforts since the tragic terrorist attacks of September 11, 2001, have focused largely on threats associated with the deliberate use of CBRN weapons, this Strategy embraces the need to engage in surveillance for WMD threats and a broader range of human, animal, and plant health challenges, including emerging infectious diseases, pandemics, agricultural threats, and food-borne illnesses. Therefore, we seek to strengthen biosurveillance capabilities to enhance all-hazards incident management by providing essential information for timely decisionmaking at all levels, whether an incident is deliberate, accidental, or naturally occurring.

Essential information is derived from a specific set of key questions that are common elements of any health emergency. These questions will be developed as part of a strategic implementation plan. This information is intended to help identify an incident, and to inform decisionmaking and time-sensitive actions at all levels to navigate health emergencies effectively. Identifying key questions and focusing our national enterprise on providing and sharing essential information is intended as a smarter, faster way to triage a health emergency and is a fundamental aspect of our Strategy.

Structure of the Strategy. This Strategy articulates an overarching goal supported by core functions. It also includes guiding principles that provide a foundation for biosurveillance activities and specific enablers to achieve a well-integrated, national biosurveillance enterprise. Through a deliberate emphasis on the identified core functions and enabling focus areas, the aim is to enhance the Nation's ability to detect, track, investigate, and navigate incidents affecting human, animal, and plant health, thereby better protecting the safety, well being, and security of the American people.

The *Guiding Principles* serve as the Strategy foundation and inform biosurveillance efforts. The Core Functions focus and prioritize our biosurveillance efforts.

The crosscutting *Enablers* are aimed at facilitating the successful implementation of our Strategy.

THE THREAT ENVIRONMENT

The deliberate use or accidental release of CBRN materials remains an enduring threat to the safety and security of the American people. One needs only to recall the terror and feelings of vulnerability caused by the anthrax letters of 2001. More recently, the Japan nuclear emergency resulting from an historic earthquake and tsunamis in 2011 reminded us of the social, economic, environmental, and health impacts of a radiological release incident.

Beyond CBRN-related concerns, the 2009-H1N1 influenza pandemic and the Severe Acute Respiratory Syndrome outbreak were clear demonstrations of the potential threat that pandemics and other emerging infectious diseases can pose to the American people. These incidents highlighted the challenges of ascertaining the course or impact of infectious diseases. Innovative developments mark the advent of threats of a new kind. Specifically, recent breakthroughs in synthetic biology offer the promise but also potentially the peril of technological progress, where the field is advancing at a staggering pace.

Our security and public health concerns are intertwined. Through science and technology developments, while it is increasingly possible to manufacture new and improved vaccines and therapeutics, it is equally possible to create genetically modified organisms that can evade our current countermeasures. In addition to various forms of biologic threats, intentional use of a chemical agent or radiologic device, along with the potential for chemical or radiologic industrial accidents, add to the spectrum of threats. Overall, the threat environment is dynamic and unpredictable. To address the challenge, this Strategy seeks to evolve our ability to detect rapidly and track incidents affecting human, animal, and plant health to save lives by informing decisionmaking at all levels.

GUIDING PRINCIPLES

Our national biosurveillance approach must address both near- and long-term information needs for a wide variety of decisionmakers and consider the context in which the overall enterprise is operating. The threat is dynamic and fiscal constraints are an everyday reality.

As such, this Strategy focuses intentionally on existing, multipurpose capabilities. In addition, our biosurveillance approach emphasizes teamwork between and within Federal departments, across all layers of government, and with private sector partners.

This Strategy also aims to prompt action that will add value for individual contributors comprising our national biosurveillance enterprise. And where resources are constrained, we aim to leverage existing, distributed capabilities more fully. The Strategy intends to add value across our national enterprise and beyond, where global health security activities are an inextricably linked and necessary aspect of strengthening of our domestic biosurveillance approach.

Specific guiding principles form the foundation of our Strategy aimed at evolving and enhancing our national biosurveillance enterprise: (1) leverage existing capabilities; (2) embrace an all-of-Nation approach; (3) add value for all participants; and (4) maintain a global health perspective.

1. *Leverage Existing Capabilities* – Taking full advantage of the resources we have, to include making key capabilities available more broadly across the enterprise, is a core principle. Extending electronic reporting of health information, including laboratory results, to public health serves as an example of rapidly communicating useful information. Another example is better integrating knowledge of

human, animal, or plant health by leveraging social media and widely available tools to facilitate rapid information sharing domestically and globally. Routine, daily use of such capabilities may be leveraged to address critical requirements in the context of an emergency.

2. *Embrace an All-of-Nation Approach* – A wide array of participants can enhance the Nation's ability to detect, track, and navigate incidents affecting human, animal, and plant health. By consciously distributing biosurveillance activities, embracing novel community information sources, and prioritizing the development of a broader array of point-of-care diagnostics, as examples, we can expand exponentially the number of "sentinels" that may detect an incident of national significance. Establishing simple protocols and institutionalizing the sharing of discrete, essential information will enable us to achieve a meaningful integration of effort.
3. *Add Value for All Participants* – With reduced resources a reality, a key tenet of our biosurveillance approach is to pursue deliberately a set of identified core functions and enablers across a distributed national architecture. This pursuit of core functions and focus areas should not radically alter current responsibilities or burden enterprise participants, and should provide a mutual benefit for participants. Even as we query others for information, or provide data ourselves, we can and should be mindful of how the exchange of information can enable efficiencies, to include leveraging the input of others to address local requirements. For example, providing information to the health care system can substantially benefit decisions regarding patient treatment, infection control measures, and hospital staffing. Maximizing the value of biosurveillance information at the community level will encourage greater participation and effectiveness across the national enterprise. There can be a value proposition for all with conscious attention.
4. *Maintain a Global Health Perspective* – Recent incidents have demonstrated consistently the global connections and our collective vulnerability to transnational health and security threats. In our interdependent world, where disease recognizes no borders, and where CBRN and other threats may emanate from abroad, our domestic biosurveillance approach must necessarily have an eye toward our shared participation in global health security. We should reinforce international connections with our national enterprise as the global biosurveillance network continues to grow.

And we should encourage other countries to integrate their surveillance and situational awareness systems and make this information available to the global community, creating a network of information nodes enhancing global response to incidents.

BIOSURVEILLANCE GOAL AND CORE FUNCTIONS

With the guiding principles as the foundation of our efforts, the *National Biosurveillance Strategy* articulates the overarching biosurveillance goal of the United States along with four core functions. Together, they promote deliberate focus and a common compass heading for our collective approach.

Our biosurveillance goal is to achieve a well-integrated national biosurveillance enterprise that saves lives by providing essential information for better decisionmaking at all levels.

Four core functions form the basis of the *National Biosurveillance Strategy*: (1) scan and discern the environment; (2) identify and integrate essential information; (3) inform and alert decisionmakers; and (4) forecast and advise potential impacts. These core functions are interrelated, multidimensional, and it is intended that they are pursued simultaneously, informing and influencing each other as part of a dynamic process. They are intended to increase incident understanding and to inform decisionmaking at all levels, even where significant ambiguity exists. Accomplishing these functions will help us to achieve the overall goal of biosurveillance.

1. Scan and Discern the Environment – This core function emphasizes attention to factors affecting the health and security of our citizens and the rapid evaluation of information to speed incident detection. Information from a range of sources, including those outside of human health or security disciplines – animal, plant, and environmental health sector information – may enhance the effectiveness of this function. The practice of actively scanning and discerning the environment involves efforts to confirm conditions and identify rapidly the emergence of new patterns or trends, while assessing their significance.
2. Identify and Integrate Essential Information – Our Strategy calls for the identification, sharing, and integration of essential information to expedite incident detection and assessment. Although all incidents have unique aspects, there are common elements of any national

public health emergency. As with a health care provider and a new patient, there are certain key questions asked to identify symptoms and narrow probable causes to assist with patient treatment. Similarly, essential information can be derived from a discrete set of key questions to speed incident detection and awareness. Information sharing and integration will be easier to achieve and to institutionalize across the national biosurveillance enterprise by focusing on these key questions.

Beyond essential information to detect and characterize an incident of national significance affecting human, animal, or plant health, our Strategy emphasizes purposeful integration across disparate information sources, including data derived from intelligence, law enforcement, environmental, plant, animal, and other relevant areas. The intent is not to share all information with all participants in the national biosurveillance enterprise, but rather to seek opportunities to add value for others by thinking more broadly about what information may be useful to enterprise participants and to share this information and analysis proactively.

By identifying, sharing, and integrating diverse information sources and expert analysis, collectively we will be more likely to identify trends signaling an incident and better able to answer key questions. The initial priority is to detect the earliest signs of potential security and health threats, then focus biosurveillance activities on the characterization and validation of the identified threat, and finally, track the threat and provide ongoing situational awareness.

3. *Alert and Inform Decisionmakers* – There exists an enduring requirement that our national biosurveillance enterprise be able to alert rapidly and inform decisionmakers of a potential incident of national significance, providing early warning and critical updates throughout any evolving incident. This function to alert and inform is iterative. And alerts do not necessarily mandate definitive action. A tension often exists between certainty and timelines for action, so it is necessary to find a balance among entities responsible for providing incident information and decisionmakers responsible for action regarding the information.
4. *Forecast and Advise Impacts* – Decisions made during an incident require an accurate comprehension of the knowable facts of the current situation and benefit from a forecast of the probable trajectory, duration, and magnitude of that incident into the future. This

forecasting capability can assist in addressing the need to act quickly to save lives and prevent negative economic consequences in certain situations, even amidst great uncertainty and ambiguity. This function involves identifying the most likely and probable impact and outcomes, and where applicable, the most dangerous and worst case scenarios. Forecasting is a cognitive process informed by facts and models, and honed with experience. Similar to economic forecasting, improvement in forecasting is not solely reliant on better modeling and simulation, but in cultivating skills derived through experience and professional development.

An efficient, effective, and well-integrated biosurveillance enterprise depends on all participants focusing their programs toward implementation of these functions. The core functions are the specific and priority areas of focus for enhancing the coordination and management of incidents of national significance affecting human, animal, and plant health, and serving as a key node in an emerging international network focused on global health. The deliberate pursuit of these carefully selected core functions is aimed at strengthening the national biosurveillance enterprise, adding value for all, and expediting decisionmaking at all levels.

ENABLERS FOR STRENGTHENING BIOSURVEILLANCE

Enabling capabilities are identified as part of our Strategy for a well-integrated national biosurveillance enterprise. Emphasis on empowering a distributed architecture and advances in relevant science and technology capabilities are a priority. These enabling capabilities are identified to facilitate the specified biosurveillance core functions. They represent ongoing focus areas to strengthen further the coordination and management of incidents of national significance affecting human, animal, and plant health.

1. Integrate Capabilities – Seek out new and creative ways to integrate biosurveillance capabilities, such as regional information sharing arrangements combining human, animal, and plant health trends. Emphasize efforts to transcend regular boundaries and across traditional organizational lines. Consider social media as a force multiplier that can empower individuals and communities to provide early warning and global situational awareness.

2. Build Capacity – Prioritize capacity building across our distributed national biosurveillance architecture, including development and use of point-of-care and multipathogen diagnostics, and the integration of fusion centers, law enforcement, intelligence, and other information collection and sharing activities. Develop a professional work force with multidisciplinary education, familiarization with information technology, and mentorship that emphasizes the four functions of biosurveillance, particularly forecasting.
3. Foster Innovation – Identify science and technology capabilities that will facilitate biosurveillance activities, including new detection and health information exchange approaches. There is substantial opportunity with the evolution of information technology to create distributed networks and empower individuals to enhance the value of biosurveillance information. In addition, encourage new thinking and the development of revised methodologies aimed at forecasting likely CBRN incidents, food-borne illness, environmental disasters, and outbreak trajectories in the absence of definitive data. As with economic and weather forecasting, there are innovative ways to combine information and known facts to project what is likely to transpire.
4. Strengthen Partnerships – Pursue biosurveillance activities that purposefully mix and match efforts and the sharing of information between and among Federal, State, local, tribal, territorial, private, nongovernmental, academic, and other national enterprise participants. Seek out an awareness of the interests of others and find ways to provide mutual benefit through existing and new partnerships and consideration of all aspects of the biosphere. Develop connections through collaborative international biosurveillance activities that will accelerate effective response to domestic and international incidents.

WAY FORWARD

A strategic implementation plan shall be completed within 120 days of the issuance of this Biosurveillance Strategy, which will include specific actions and activity scope, designated roles and responsibilities, and a mechanism for evaluating progress.

During the development of the implementation plan, we will delineate the key questions that identify biosurveillance essential information for decisionmaking. Current and planned activities and capabilities-based planning will complement the Presidential Policy Directive-8 – "*National Preparedness*" implementation process, where biosurveillance is identified as a key capability for national preparedness.

CONCLUSION

Protecting the health and safety of the American people through a well-integrated national biosurveillance enterprise is a top national security priority. It requires that we focus on core functions to make further progress. It also necessitates that we embrace an all-of-Nation approach and indeed a global health security intent, as the effects of any deliberate CBRN attack or accident, or emerging infectious disease, can transcend national borders. There exists an imperative that we expand our efforts to detect rapidly a potential incident of national significance affecting human, animal, or plant health, whether resulting from a bioterror attack or other CBRN threat, an emerging infectious disease, pandemic, or a food-borne illness. Rapid detection is critical to save lives and improve incident outcomes, and the United States serves as a key node as part of an international network of biosurveillance centers across the globe.

Our National Strategy for Biosurveillance seeks to leverage existing capabilities across the Nation yet emphasizes a discrete focus on specified core functions. It articulates that essential information can be derived from a specific set of questions to speed the detection of a deliberate or accidental CBRN incident or naturally occurring disease outbreak. This Strategy further articulates that when the collection and sharing of this essential information is prioritized, decisionmaking can be expedited at all levels of government and beyond.

This is the essence of our approach. While other activities are integral to everyday local biosurveillance efforts that can and should continue, our Strategy calls for a national focus on fewer issues so that more can be achieved collectively. Our approach also seeks to inspire new thinking and revised methodologies to "forecast" that which we cannot yet prove, so that timely decisions can be made to save lives and reduce impacts during an emergency incident.

This is our Strategy. It is our plan of action to protect the health, well being, and safety of the American people as part of the global community.

End Note

[1] Homeland Security Presidential Directive-21 remains in effect and defines biosurveillance as the process of active data-gathering with appropriate analysis and interpretation of biosphere data that might relate to disease activity and threats to human or animal health – whether infectious, toxic, metabolic, or otherwise, and regardless of intentional or natural origin – in order to achieve early warning of health threats, early detection of health events, and overall situational awareness of disease activity.

In: National Biosurveillance Strategy ... ISBN: 978-1-62948-994-0
Editor: Amanda Wendell

Chapter 2

NATIONAL BIOSURVEILLANCE SCIENCE AND TECHNOLOGY ROADMAP*

Biosurveillance Science and Technology Working Group

June 14, 2013

Dear Colleague,

I am pleased to transmit the National Biosurveillance Science and Technology Roadmap, which identifies and prioritizes research and development (R&D) needs with the goal of giving decision makers at all levels of government more accurate and timely information when biological incidents threaten health.

Such incidents—whether the result of natural evolutionary causes, accidental releases or exposures, or malevolent activities—have the potential to erupt suddenly and evolve quickly. Surveillance can be key to predicting and even preventing such incidents, and can help minimize the impacts of incidents that cannot be prevented.

The Roadmap builds upon the National Strategy for Biosurveillance, published in July 2012, which recognized that a well-integrated national biosurveillance enterprise can save lives by providing essential information for

---

* This report was released by the Executive Office of the President, National Science and Technology Council, Office of Science and Technology Policy, June 2013.

better decision making. Drafted by the interagency Biosurveillance Science and Technology Working Group under the National Science and Technology Council's Committee on Homeland and National Security, the Roadmap identifies R&D priorities to enable the Core Functions of the Strategy.

The Obama Administration is committed to working toward the achievement of these high-priority R&D objectives and to realizing the integrated biosurveillance enterprise called for in the Strategy. Success will require coordination across Federal organizations, academia, industry, and the international community. The benefit for the health and security of all Americans and indeed all the world's people makes the needed effort extremely worthwhile.

Sincerely,

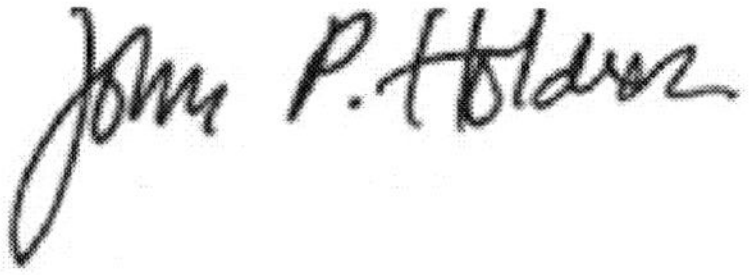

John P. Holdren
Director

ACRONYMS AND ABBREVIATIONS

APHIS	Animal and Plant Health Inspection Service
BDRD	Biological Defense Research and Development
BIWAC	Biosurveillance Indications and Warning Analytic Community
BSP	Biosurveillance Portal
BST WG	Biosurveillance Science and Technology Working Group
BSV	Biosurveillance
CAPS	Cooperative Agricultural Pest Survey
CDC	Centers for Disease Control and Prevention
DHS	Department of Homeland Security
DoD	Department of Defense
DOI	Department of the Interior
DTRA	Defense Threat Reduction Agency
EIP	Emerging Infection Programs
EROS	Earth Resources Observation and Science

ESSENCE	Electronic Surveillance System for Early Notification of Community-based Epidemics
FDA	Food and Drug Administration
HHS	U.S. Department of Health and Human Services
HSPD	Homeland Security Presidential Directive
ICLN	Integrated Consortium of Laboratory Networks
LRN	Laboratory Response Network
NAHLN	National Animal Health Laboratory Network
NAHMS	National Animal Health Monitoring System
NBIC	National Biosurveillance Integration Center
NBIS	National Biosurveillance Integration System
NCMI	National Center for Medical Intelligence
NEON	National Ecological Observatory Network
NGDS	Next Generation Diagnostics System
NIH	National Institutes of Health
NOAA	National Oceanographic and Atmospheric Administration
NPDN	National Plant Diagnostic Network
NSF	National Science Foundation
NSIV	National Swine Influenza Virus Surveillance Program
NSTC	National Science and Technology Council
NWHC	National Wildlife Health Center
OSTP	Office of Science and Technology Policy
PHAA	Public Health Actionable Assays
PHEMCE	Public Health Emergency Medical Countermeasure Enterprise
POC	Point of Care
POCTRN	Point of Care Technologies Research Network
PON	Point of Need
R&D	Research and Development
RAPIDD	Research and Policy for Infectious Disease Dynamics
Roadmap	Biosurveillance Science and Technology Roadmap
S&T	Science and Technology
Strategy	National Strategy for Biosurveillance
USDA	U.S. Department of Agriculture
USGS	U.S. Geological Survey

EXECUTIVE SUMMARY

The *National Strategy for Biosurveillance* (*Strategy*), published in July 2012, calls for "a coordinated approach that brings together Federal, state, local, and tribal governments; the private sector; nongovernmental organizations; and international partners" to enhance existing biosurveillance capabilities and, where necessary, develop new ones that provide decision makers and responders with the essential information they need to mitigate impacts of threats to health and associated economic, societal, and political consequences. The *Strategy* recognizes that a well-integrated national biosurveillance enterprise can saves lives by providing essential information for better decision making at all levels.

The interagency Biosurveillance Science and Technology Working Group (BST WG), chartered in May 2012, was established under the Subcommittee on Biological Defense Research and Development of the National Science and Technology Council's Committee on Homeland and National Security to develop national biosurveillance research and development priorities to enable the Core Functions of the *Strategy*.

The BST WG established four sub-working groups, each focused on addressing a distinct but interrelated aspect of biosurveillance science and technology: aberration detection; risk anticipation; threat identification and characterization; and information sharing, integration, and analysis. Together, the four groups identified the following high-priority research and development objectives to be prioritized in this period of limited resources:

- Establish baseline levels of community and ecosystem risks, threats, and health;
- Identify causes of aberrations from normal at the ecosystem, organism, reservoir, vector, and host nexus;
- Identify indicators that are associated with potential outbreaks and develop models using these indicators to assist in better decision making at all levels;
- Enhance information integration, analysis, and sharing platforms for improved situational awareness of biosurveillance information at all levels, including with international partners, as appropriate;
- Further develop technological solutions that integrate and analyze electronic health information, while protecting private information, to better inform health decision making;

- Identify and evaluate the utility of novel sources of biosurveillance information, such as social media;
- Improve exposure assessment and diagnostic capability, especially at the point of care, to enable accurate and timely collection of information for early detection and situational awareness throughout an incident; and
- Improve identification and characterization of known and unknown health threats.

Achievement of these high-priority research and development objectives and realization of the integrated biosurveillance enterprise called for in the *Strategy* will require coordination across Federal organizations, academia, industry, and the international community.

SECTION 1. INTRODUCTION

"A well-integrated, national biosurveillance enterprise is a national security imperative."

–National Strategy for Biosurveillance, July 2012.

Background

Threats to human, animal, and plant health have the potential for significant economic, social, and political consequences. These consequences can be minimized by quick, well-informed action; the sooner a threat is detected and understood, the faster a response can be mounted and the threat's effects minimized. The *National Strategy for Biosurveillance* (*Strategy)*, published in July 2012, calls for "a coordinated approach that brings together Federal, state, local, and tribal governments; the private sector; nongovernmental organizations; and international partners" to enhance existing biosurveillance[1] capabilities and, where necessary, develop new ones that provide decision makers and responders with the essential information they need to mitigate impacts of threats to health—including the health of people, plants, domestic animals, and wildlife—and to food security and agriculture.

The *Implementation Plan for the National Strategy for Biosurveillance* (*Implementation Plan*) identifies and prioritizes actions needed to achieve the goals of the *Strategy*. One such action is the development of "...a research and development (R&D) roadmap that encourages innovation and collaboration in priority R&D areas...and addresses key scientific and technological gaps to strengthen the biosurveillance enterprise."

This National Biosurveillance (BSV) Science and Technology (S&T) Roadmap (*Roadmap*) identifies and prioritizes the R&D efforts needed to provide decision makers at all levels with the accurate and timely information needed to develop effective responses to incidents that threaten health. The R&D objectives in this *Roadmap* are designed to facilitate the accomplishment of the core functions and actions identified in the *Strategy* and *Implementation Plan*, respectively. Consistent with the *Strategy* and Homeland Security Presidential Directive (HSPD)-21 entitled *Public Health and Medical Preparedness*, this *Roadmap* focuses on S&T for anticipating significant health incidents involving naturally occurring, accidental, or manmade threats; rapidly and accurately identifying and characterizing incidents that occur; and effectively integrating, sharing, and analyzing the information available at each stage. Achieving the S&T objectives in this *Roadmap* will permit better decision making during an incident, resulting in improved mitigation, response, and recovery[2] that may ultimately save lives and improve health.

This *Roadmap* also identifies areas of potential department and agency collaboration to better leverage existing funding streams.

METHODOLOGY

To create this *Roadmap*, the BST WG was established under the Subcommittee on Biological Defense Research and Development of the National Science and Technology Council's Committee on Homeland and National Security. The BST WG established four sub-working groups to explore four S&T focus areas in support of the *Strategy's* Core Functions:

Aberration detection – Define and prioritize R&D needed to establish the baseline condition of the environment and/or human (including vulnerable subpopulations), animal, or plant populations that is sufficiently robust to permit rapid identification of aberrant incidents to drive preparedness and timely, focused investigation.

Risk anticipation – Define and prioritize R&D needed to identify antecedent conditions and characterize complex interactions that permit prediction of an impending natural or intentional incident and to forecast impacts from such incidents.

Threat identification and characterization – Define and prioritize R&D needed to ensure exposures and health threats are identified rapidly and accurately and can be sufficiently characterized to provide needed information to decision makers, including responders and healthcare providers.

Information integration, analysis, and sharing – Define and prioritize R&D needed to enable improved integration, sharing, and analysis of BSV data in near real-time and in a format that provides essential information to decision makers, including responders and healthcare providers.

Each of the four sub-working groups was tasked to develop a baseline of the current state of BSV programs relevant to their focus area. This baseline served as a foundation to conduct a gap analysis with respect to the *Strategy* and identify priority S&T needs. Rather than describe all ongoing BSV-related programs identified by this process, this *Roadmap* highlights some representative Federal Government activities within each focus area.

Although many of the concepts and gaps described in this *Roadmap* have application across all hazards, this report focuses on biological threats to national security, including known and emerging infectious disease agents with potential to significantly affect the health of the environment, plants, animals, and humans around the globe, whether naturally occurring or released accidentally or intentionally.

SECTION 2. FOUNDATIONS: ABERRATION DETECTION

Key Research Priorities

- Establish baseline levels of community and ecosystem risks, threats, and health
- Enhance methods and tools to rapidly detect aberrations from the baseline

Background

Watching for and detecting aberrations from baseline conditions are the first essential steps to assessing and anticipating health risks and threats; identifying and characterizing those threats; and integrating, analyzing, and sharing information about the threats, as called for in the *Strategy*. Effective decision making relies on detecting aberrations from baseline conditions (e.g., a rapid increase in the number of influenza cases) sufficient to warrant a threat alert and the recommendation of precautionary or preventive measures (e.g., attention to hand washing and vaccination for influenza or mass prophylaxis for a bioterrorism event).

Aberration detection requires an ability to reliably distinguish a valid signal from background noise and qualitatively characterize and interpret the significance of that signal. Of course, in order to detect potentially threatening aberrations from "normal conditions" it is necessary to know what is "normal"—the baseline state of the environment or of human, animal, or plant populations against which aberrations can be measured. Moreover, this capacity must be dynamic and context-sensitive; what is normal now or in one circumstance may not be in the future or under different circumstances.

Current approaches to surveillance have variable accuracy and timeliness and in some cases detect aberrations only quantitatively without the necessary qualitative characterization.

Most quantitative detections require expert evaluations before action should be taken. For example, syndromic surveillance systems may identify illness clusters early (before diagnoses are confirmed) and alert public health agencies, but the systems do not necessarily determine the cause, thus requiring additional subject-matter expertise to make sense of a given alert and drive subsequent action.

Qualitative characterization is straightforward if the surveillance data are specific (e.g., results from influenza A laboratory tests), but can be quite limited if the data are non-specific (e.g., spike in emergency department visits for fever or symptoms that are shared by multiple diseases).

Given the current prevalence of non-specific surveillance data, the development of methods for qualitative characterization is critical. Thus, any efforts to improve aberration detection should go beyond statistical improvements in detection accuracy to include qualitative analysis of aberrations.

Current Programs

Multiple Federal departments and agencies are working toward improved aberration detection, with some programs focused in particular on characterization of normal background. These efforts include the following:

Human Microbiome Project: The National Institutes of Health's (NIH) Human Microbiome Project[3] aims to characterize microbial communities found at multiple human body sites (e.g., nasal passages, oral cavities, skin, gastrointestinal tract, and urogenital tract) and look for correlations between changes in the microbiome and human health and disease. Initiatives include developing reference sets of microbial genome sequences; characterizing through molecular approaches the relationship between changes in the human microbiome and human health and disease; development of new technologies and tools for computational analysis; and establishment of resource repositories (e.g., reference strains, data, software).

National Ecological Observatory Network (NEON): The National Science Foundation (NSF) is supporting the construction and operation of NEON is a continental-scale ecological observation and research platform designed to enable the assessment of both the human causes and biological consequences of environmental change.

NEON will provide data and data products needed to improve our understanding of and ability to forecast the impacts of climate change, land use change, and invasive species on ecosystem structure and function – specifically including biodiversity, biogeochemistry, ecohydrology, and infectious disease.

These data and high-level data products will be available in close to real-time and will provide a regional to continental scale environmental baseline and the ability to detect changes from that baseline.

National Wildlife Health Center (NWHC): The Department of the Interior (DOI) U.S. Geological Survey's (USGS) NWHC conducts long-term monitoring and surveillance for wildlife health and disease detection and prevention in both aquatic and terrestrial environments. The NWHC provides diagnostic and disease research on wildlife; leads diseases investigations; participates in emergency response to medium and large-scale wildlife die-offs; and provides education, training, and outreach to wildlife personnel at both national and international levels.

National Animal Health Monitoring System (NAHMS): The U.S. Department of Agriculture's (USDA) Animal and Plant Health Inspection Service (APHIS) NAHMS[4] has been in place for over 20 years. The NAHMS Program Unit conducts national studies to provide essential information on livestock and poultry health and management to decision makers, including producers, researchers, and policymakers.

Each animal group is studied at regular intervals, providing up-to-date and trend information needed to monitor animal health, support trade decisions, assess research and product development needs, answer questions for consumers, and set policy.

Capability Needs

The following capabilities are needed to strengthen aberration detection:

- Surveillance methodologies that integrate traditional monitoring (i.e., pathogen, environmental, health) with background data (i.e., meteorological and population dynamics) that may influence risk

New modeling and ecological forecasting approaches have the potential to enhance the effectiveness of current strategies for predicting the likelihood of disease outbreaks and determining likely impacts when a threat is detected. For example, Hantavirus is endemic in the southwestern United States, where it is carried by deer mice.

Research into the factors that determine the population dynamics of mice, such as multiyear patterns of rainfall, now enable public health agencies to issue warnings in years where the risk of human infection is high because of predicted increases in mouse populations.

While imperfect, this integrated surveillance has the potential to dramatically reduce human infections as well as improve the speed of diagnosis and efficacy of treatment.

- Ability to detect early warning signs of changes occurring at different and changing spatial and temporal scales

Automated aberration detection approaches often depend on data extraction and/or translation of foreign language reports—endeavors that would be greatly improved by advances in computer science and, in particular, the field of statistical anomaly detection in low signal-to-noise environments. While improvements are made in these areas of basic science, BSV could benefit from lessons learned by researchers in other fields that also rely on weak-signal extraction, such as sonar and radar detection of submarines and missiles.

- Advancements in data sharing and integration and communication technologies including assessment methods

Equally important to the detection of aberrations is the need to integrate and analyze the monitored data and communicate the information to decision makers rapidly and securely. For example, early recognition of disease through the examination of data from electronic medical records has public health value only if that signal is available to decision makers in time to influence a response that can mitigate the impacts of the disease.

Cooperation among Federal and non-federal stakeholders, including the scientific community and public and private healthcare providers, is essential to achieve an efficient and reliable surveillance system.

- Education and training to meet anticipated needs for BSV professionals

New and non-traditional data collection and processing techniques have transformed the art and science of epidemiologic analysis. That in turn has increased the need for a more specialized workforce skilled in the application of these new and emerging capabilities.

In order to prepare the next generation of scientists and engineers for successful careers as BSV professionals, education and training opportunities should be developed.

Research Priorities

Based on the capability needs described above and analysis of current programs, the following broad research priorities are proposed, with accompanying specific objectives:

- Establish baseline levels of community and ecosystem risks, threats, and health
    - Assess baseline exposures to endemic, occupational, and environmental threats;
    - Expand spatial and temporal mapping of endemic and epidemic disease;
    - Determine levels of immune (natural and vaccine-derived) protection for various populations;
    - Understand human behaviors and animal behaviors associated with health and illness and demographic trends; and

    - Understand pathway issues associated with trade and movement of people (e.g., smuggling and unintentional transport of pathogens or pests with plant or animal products).
- Enhance methods and tools to rapidly detect aberrations from the baseline
    - Develop statistical or mathematical algorithms to quickly and reliably distinguish a valid threat signal from background conditions;
    - Improve language processing and parsing tools;
    - Differentiate (temporal scale) between changes of immediate concern (e.g., influenza, foot-and-mouth disease) and those that have a large scale effect but spread more slowly (e.g., sudden oak death, fungal infections in bats and bees);
    - Assess state-of-the-art in aberration detection methods and tools applied in other sectors (e.g., intelligence, financial markets, credit industry) and evaluate how they might be leveraged or applied to BSV applications; and
    - Improve qualitative characterization of aberrations through targeted education and training of the next generation of BSV professionals.

Summary and Conclusion

Continued improvements in high-dimensional analysis of health data, integrated with data describing environmental factors, vector distribution, and other factors, can facilitate rapid detection and characterization. These approaches have considerable potential for predicting, detecting, and characterizing aberrations in a way that could transform how surveillance data and related information is presented and used by decision makers.

This reality underscores the need for an approach that rationally guides efforts to define a complex and dynamic baseline and focuses S&T investments on those anomaly detection methods and tools that will be most effective in achieving the goals in the *Strategy*. Similarly, improvements in the integration, analysis, and sharing of information among appropriately trained stakeholders can ensure that monitored data has the greatest impact on disease mitigation.

SECTION 3. RISK ANTICIPATION

Key Research Priorities

- Sustain R&D aimed at improving understanding of determinants of disease emergence and reemergence
- Focus on R&D relating to forecasting technologies and models that consider ecological and evolutionary drivers of disease behavior
- Connect non-invasive data-gathering tools to other types of surveillance data to improve the ability to detect antecedent conditions and the earliest indications of a significant incident

Background

Globalization and ecological pressures are increasing the risk that a biological incident of national significance, such as the emergence of a novel infectious agent and/or a global pandemic, will occur. An important component of mitigating the consequences of such an incident is to anticipate when and where it may occur, enabling a more timely and well-informed response.

The earlier a risk is anticipated and an actionable warning is broadcast, the greater the likelihood that a health threat can be prevented or its impacts significantly reduced. Risk anticipation requires the means to predict when an incident is likely to occur and to forecast its potential impacts on a given population. Technologies that help anticipate the risk seek to identify, measure, and analyze the many factors that set the conditions for, or directly influence, emergence of threats.

Emergence of many natural diseases is directly affected by easily measured environmental conditions, such as when isolated host environments are encroached upon. However, the complex patterns and interactions among hosts, vectors, the pathogens themselves, and the environment are not easily elucidated.

For example, pathogenic determinants in the microbial world develop as a result of myriad biological and ecological pressures. The interaction between microbes and human and animal populations is affected by climate, the presence of pharmaceuticals, chemical additives and compounds, and social behaviors.

Changes caused by those interactions occur with varying speed and scope to set the conditions for disease emergence. In addition, there remain a number of uncertainties about which pathogenic changes act to increase virulence, host range, or other factors.

While there are ongoing R&D projects to understand these complex interactions, realizing the *Strategy's* goals will require strategic integration of efforts including near- and long-term S&T investments.

Current Programs

As described in Section 2, multiple Federal departments and agencies fund efforts to enhance baseline knowledge of genetics, molecular biology, proteomics, ecology, and epidemiology of known and emerging threats affecting the ecosystem, humans, animals, and plants to determine their relevance to national security and health. Traditionally, research has focused on retrospective evaluation to better understand data requirements and identify determinant variables from existing outbreaks. In order to prospectively assess current sparse data and provide projections of potential disease risks in an anticipatory manner, both pre- and post-incident, research priorities must be better articulated and coordinated among government, academia, industry, and non-governmental organizations.

Infectious Disease Emergence and Transmission: The joint NSF/NIH Ecology and Evolution of Infectious Disease program[5] supports efforts to understand the underlying ecological and biological mechanisms that govern relationships between human-induced environmental changes and the emergence and transmission of infectious disease. Similarly, NIH and the Department of Homeland Security (DHS) support a cooperative program called Research and Policy for Infectious Disease Dynamics (RAPIDD)[6]. Through an extensive series of workshops, working groups, and postdoctoral fellowships designed to address critical challenges, RAPIDD seeks to understand which models and modeling approaches will facilitate adequate operational capacity; how models relate with one another and with data of various quality and scale; and how the needs of decision makers can be characterized and addressed through modeling. RAPIDD focuses on improving the modeling of foreign animal diseases and zoonotic infections, aiming to make models more reliable and relevant to policy makers preparing for or responding to outbreaks. Finally, the NIH Models of Infectious Disease Agent Study is a transdisciplinary consortium of research groups with the mission of developing computational, mathematical, and statistical models of infectious disease dynamics and assisting decision makers to prepare for, detect, and respond to infectious disease threats.

Current technologies and tools to recognize and visualize early indicators include remotely-sensed imagery, common operating pictures, and disease modeling/forecasting. Federally funded modeling research on specific, highly infectious diseases, such as novel respiratory diseases with pandemic potential, is currently most useful for mitigation and response. Some success has been achieved in computationally assisted methods for predicting disease outbreaks. This success remains in the realm of disease risk mapping (e.g., ecological niche modeling), typically of vector-borne disease where meteorological and environmental conditions are the principal drivers and the diseases recur with some regularity in the same general location (e.g., cholera, Rift Valley fever, Hantavirus). In contrast, the current state of science does not allow for accurate predictions of the emergence of novel diseases or of the reemergence of diseases for which no regular cycle of emergence is known. Satellite instruments are powerful non-invasive data-gathering tools and are currently the most suitable tools to identify environmental and climatic precursors to infectious disease outbreaks. Current satellite operations may make it possible to identify early (or predictive) indications of biological threats by capturing changes in the relationships among human, animal, and plant populations, such as population density, interactions and migration, and environmental conditions. Although these efforts present promise in the near-term for informing decision making, true predictive capability will require maturation of the science behind current modeling methods and continued collaboration among government, academia, industry, and non-governmental organizations.

Global Weather and Climate Models: The National Oceanographic and Atmospheric Administration (NOAA) National Centers for Environmental Prediction runs global weather and climate models and makes global weather and climate forecasts. It leverages its expertise in the use of model and monitoring data to guide informed decision-making about human diseases by, for example, investigating the relationship between climate and incidence of meningitis. NOAA's Center for Satellite Applications and Research—part of the National Environmental Satellite, Data, and Information Service—develops health-related satellite data sets and products to help inform decisions relating to such diseases as malaria and dengue fever.

Earth Resources Observation and Science (EROS) Center[7]*:* In partnership with the National Aeronautics and Space Administration, the USGS's EROS Center has been the steward and distributor of Landsat satellite data for over

40 years. The Landsat series of satellite missions has collected imagery of the Earth's surface since 1972, providing the most comprehensive record of the global landmass ever assembled. The EROS mission includes developing, implementing, and operating remote-sensing-based land-change monitoring, assessment, and prediction capabilities needed to address science objectives at all levels – within the USGS, across the Federal Government, and around the world. Landsat data are extremely valuable for a range of applications that contribute to science, environmental monitoring, and homeland security.

Federal departments and agencies are also aggressively assessing the role of technologies, such as social media, in characterizing disease emergence, reemergence, and nefarious exploitation of biological agents. To date, however, these efforts are limited to intelligence data triage, post-incident analysis of signal-to-noise relationships, and veracity of reporting with an eye toward situational awareness.

National Center for Medical Intelligence (NCMI): The NCMI, a component of the Department of Defense's (DoD) Defense Intelligence Agency, develops structured intelligence warning approaches to disease events of national significance (intentionally caused or naturally occurring), leveraging disparate open-source data, intelligence derived from National Technical Means, epidemiologic expertise, and intelligence tradecraft to move the intelligence warning capability temporally closer to the origins of an incident with the ultimate goal of warning prior to the emergence of a disease incident. Based on decades of basic data gathering and disease reporting, NCMI aims to expand its capacity to quickly identify abnormal disease occurrences and behavior globally. In partnership with the DoD Chemical Biological Defense Program and multiple Federal non-Title-50 partners, NCMI is exploring computational modeling, semantic fusion, entity resolution, link analysis, and molecular biological techniques that present some degree of promise in achieving a predictive capacity for the intelligence community.

PREDICT: PREDICT is a project of the U.S. Agency for International Development's Emerging Pandemic Threats Program that is building global surveillance to detect and prevent spillover of pathogens of pandemic potential that can move between wildlife and people. PREDICT has built a broad coalition of international partners to discover, detect, and monitor diseases at the wildlife-human interface using a risk-based approach that includes integrating digital sensing and on-the-ground surveillance at critical points for disease emergence. PREDICT is at the cutting-edge of recent technological advances allowing for rapid detection and diagnosis of high-risk viral families in all resource settings.

Capability Needs

Predicting the emergence of animal and plant diseases and zoonoses and forecasting the outcomes of their occurrence are significant scientific challenges. The principal needs to better forecast significant disease events and anticipate their risks include:

- Understanding of antecedent conditions at appropriate spatial and temporal scales

The science of predicting discontinuous change in complex systems is relative immature—a challenge exacerbated by a relative paucity of data. In contrast to the physical sciences, in which systems and relevant variables can be enumerated and characterized in functionally closed systems, biological incidents occur in open systems, making the process of identifying and limiting relevant variables a daunting task.

- Ability to forecast the dynamics of novel disease emergence or the exploitation of biological agents by adversaries

The ability to forecast impacts of the emergence of a novel disease or an intentionally released agent begins with having some fundamental understanding of environmental and behavioral factors that have predictive influence on an agent's behavior, including the movement of a human or animal population within the environment. Further, rapid characterization of the at-risk population, whether by direct knowledge (e.g., census data) or remote analysis (e.g., human geography/human terrain analysis), as well as the agent's transmissibility, mode of transmission, and generation time are key contributors to forecast impact. With respect to deliberate releases of pathogens, physical parameters of dispersal and the behavior of threat agents when aerosolized under various environmental conditions can illuminate the likely upper and lower bounds of the initial affected population. Basic epidemiology can then inform secondary transmission in the event an agent is contagious.

Research Priorities

Based on the capability needs described above and analysis of current programs, the following broad research priorities are proposed, with accompanying specific objectives:

- Sustain R&D efforts aimed at improving understanding of determinants of disease emergence and reemergence, including ecological and evolutionary factors that promote the ability of organisms to move to new host-species (e.g., swine/avian influenza to humans) and acquire antimicrobial resistance
  - Develop improved molecular approaches (genomics, meta-genomics, proteomics, nondestructive sequencing) to elucidate exposure causes and effects, and host/vector/reservoir-specific molecular-level relationships and interactions in the context of known and, ultimately, newly emergent biological threats;
  - Integrate the vast array of wildlife data (e.g., harmful algal blooms, fish kills, marine mammal strandings, migration) and environmental data (e.g., air quality, toxic exposures, public health surveys) collected by governmental agencies, academia, and industry, and merge these data into geographical and temporal visualization tools; and
  - Improve linkage between this basic research and the applied model-development research as described below.
- Focus on R&D relating to forecasting technologies and models that consider ecological and evolutionary drivers of disease behavior
  - Advance modeling R&D and analytical frameworks for specific classes of incidents (e.g., influenza versus cholera versus intentional release scenarios); and
  - Improve operational quality through rigorous testing of the reliability and validity of models.
- Connect non-invasive data-gathering tools to other types of surveillance data to improve the ability to detect antecedent conditions and the earliest indications of a significant incident
  - Characterize conditions, demographics, and environmental factors that can inform the earliest possible warning and projection of impact, as well as points of intervention to positively affect projected impacts;

- Integrate emerging remote sensing capabilities/analysis (such as biological, chemical, and hyperspectral) with fixed, distributed autonomous or semi-autonomous surveillance platforms and conventional molecular biological tools to characterize and ultimately predict spatially and temporally important environmental variables that influence disease emergence within ecosystems, including humans;
- Examine current coverage and capabilities of ground-based, in situ sensors for detecting threats, and enhance efficiency or expand, as appropriate and feasible;
- Develop individual exposure assessment technologies, such as pre-symptomatic exposure biomarkers and individual dosimeters, to more rapidly and accurately detect exposures.

Summary and Conclusion

New foundational science and operational capabilities are needed to develop the ability to predict the impacts and risks posed by emerging diseases. Robust characterization of antecedent environmental conditions and the molecular dynamics of ecology-reservoir-host-pathogen interactions that can drive pathogenesis are essential to attain a true predictive capacity. Ultimately, such capabilities should be able to predict whether a health incident anywhere in the world will progress to one of regional, national, or international significance.

SECTION 4. THREAT IDENTIFICATION AND CHARACTERIZATION

Key Research Priorities

- Development of rapid, reliable next generation detection and diagnostic capabilities
- Development of new tools and methodologies to improve collection, preservation, transport, and preparation of clinical and non-diagnostic samples

- Development of instrumentation and large data-set-processing capabilities to rapidly identify characteristics of agents

Background

Health is essential to national security. Health threats for human populations pose obvious security risks, but diseases in plant and animal populations can also pose serious security risks, including disruption of the food supply and commerce, with potentially long-lasting human health and economic impacts. Early detection of such threats can support determinations of the population exposed, diagnosis and treatment decisions, and containment of the threat. Strengthened laboratory and field capabilities are needed to recognize potential health threats as early as possible.

Diagnostic tests provide crucial information to surveillance programs in a variety of operational contexts, including U.S. laboratory networks and U.S. reference diagnostic laboratories associated with the World Health Organization, the United Nations Food and Agriculture Organization, and the World Organization for Animal Health (formerly known as the Office International des Epizooties). It is critical that technologies and methodologies to enable rapid and accurate identification and characterization of health threats are broadly available and fully functional.

Current Programs

A number of programs today contribute to the Nation's capacity to identify and characterize health threats. Several representative programs are described below, categorized by some of the overarching identification and characterization challenges they address.

- *Diagnosis of disease at point of care (POC) and point of need (PON):* Infectious disease diagnostic testing generally occurs in fixed-site clinical laboratories. Typically, clinicallaboratory-based diagnostic platforms are not cost effective or rugged enough for use in POC/PON settings where treatment can be initiated sooner. While several POC/PON tests exist for initial patient testing, they are limited by poor sensitivity or specificity and generally require a confirmatory clinical laboratory test result prior to treatment. Advanced POC/PON testing platforms with sensitivity and specificity similar to those used in clinical laboratories are becoming available for limited resource settings; however, they remain high complexity tests and continue to require a trained laboratory clinician to ensure reliable results, limiting their global adoption.

Point of Care Technologies Research Network (POCTRN): The NIH POCTRN drives the development of appropriate POC technologies through collaborative efforts that merge scientific, engineering, and technological capabilities with clinical need. The POCTRN is developing technologies for the diagnosis, screening, treatment, and monitoring of a variety of diseases. A major goal of POCTRN is higher quality care at reduced cost, with a shift in focus from specialized care for the treatment of late-stage disease to an emphasis on patient-centered approaches and coordinated care teams that promote wellness and effective disease management.

DoD Next Generation Diagnostics System (NGDS): The DoD NGDS is an incrementally acquired family of systems intended to provide an enhanced diagnostic capability from the laboratory to the field in support the DoD and its U.S. Government partners. Short-term investments will focus on the acquisition of a commercial off-theshelf diagnostic system suitable for use in field and mobile laboratories and development of Food and Drug Administration (FDA)-cleared biological agent in vitro diagnostic assays. Long-term efforts will focus on the development of far-forward diagnostic capabilities and diagnostics for chemical, biological, radiological, and nuclear threats. Common themes throughout all increments of the NGDS program are alignment with therapeutics and the pursuit of common materiel solutions for endemic infectious disease diagnostics, and environmental sample analysis for public health and biological defense applications.

- Detection of threat agents in non-diagnostic samples using field-based and laboratory systems: A number of laboratory and disease-tracking networks are available to perform confirmatory testing of suspected disease threats (such as suspicious powders or animal droppings) and to detect disease trends in animals and plants. For example, the Centers for Disease Control and Prevention's (CDC) Laboratory Response Network (LRN) is an integrated system of state and local public health, Federal, military, and international laboratories that operate continuously for laboratory identification of threats associated with terrorism and other public health emergencies. Similarly, USDA and USGS reference laboratories are members of diagnostic laboratory networks such as the National Animal Health Laboratory Network8 (NAHLN) and the National Plant Diagnostic Network (NPDN)9, which provide rapid detection and confirmatory diagnoses of known threats to plants and animals.

Federally Funded Biological Detection Systems: There are several detection systems currently deployed to conduct continuous surveillance for biological threats in non-diagnostic samples by Federal departments and agencies and private-sector organizations. Examples include: DHS' BioWatch Program; DoD's Installation Protection Program and Joint Biological Point Detection System for wide-area detection of aerosol threats; the Environmental Protection Agency's Water Security Initiative to detect contamination of drinking water distribution systems; NOAA's Harmful Algal Bloom forecast network; the U.S. Postal Service Biohazard Detection System used to screen mail in U.S. postal facilities across the Nation; and DOI USGS' Migratory Wild Bird Disease Surveillance Program using migratory, genetic, and immunological data to identify likely routes of virus introduction, and prioritizing migratory bird species for sampling based on their potential to transmit highly pathogenic avian influenza into North America.

Public Health Actionable AssaysTM (PHAA): The PHAA effort sets stringent assay performance evaluation and validation requirements for both non-diagnostic samples as well as clinical samples within the LRN member laboratories; PHAA ensures clinical samples are compliant with FDA regulations for in vitro diagnostic use. The evaluation and performance requirements were determined through an interagency effort. Assays that achieve this level of performance provide the high confidence identification results necessary in the public health community to inform early decision making.

Cooperative Agricultural Pest Survey (CAPS): USDA's APHIS leverages efforts by state departments of agriculture, universities, and industry partners in annual surveys targeting specific exotic plant pests that threaten U.S. agricultural and/or natural settings by funding a network of cooperators that participate in the CAPS program and conduct surveys and testing. The NPDN is a strong partner with Federal and state programs to provide a distributed nationwide network of public agricultural institutions to quickly detect high consequence pests and pathogens using federally validated methods and immediately report them to appropriate responders and decision makers.

National Swine Influenza Virus (NSIV) Surveillance Program: USDA and CDC initiated a swine influenza virus surveillance pilot project in 2008 to track the epidemiology and ecology of swine influenza virus in swine and human infections. Under this pilot project, when the human pandemic influenza outbreak occurred in April 2009, CDC quickly shared human H1N1 virus isolates with USDA, allowing USDA to rapidly develop, validate, and deploy to the NAHLN an A(H1N1)pdm09-specific diagnostic polymerase chain reaction assay. The surveillance pilot was expanded and then modified into the NSIV surveillance program to (1) monitor genetic evolution of swine influenza virus; (2) make swine influenza virus isolates available for research and an objective database for genetic analysis of these isolates and related information; and (3) select proper isolates for the development of relevant diagnostic reagents and vaccine seed stocks.

- Rapid characterization of emerging and novel threats: Laboratory characterization of a novel disease-causing agent involves the collection of high confidence genotypic and phenotypic information, such as those related to critical pathogen properties (e.g., phylogeny, virulence, growth, morphology, pathogenicity, viability, transmissibility, antibiotic susceptibility, and functional genomics); host immune response and early disease markers; microbial source identification indicators; and ecological adaptations. Data derived from this type of in-depth analysis informs medical countermeasure development and response.

Technologies for Rapid Characterization and Identification: CDC's Rapid Response & Advanced Technology Laboratory, in conjunction with the Biotechnology Core Facility and Office of Public Health Preparedness and Response, is facilitating an interagency multi-tiered technology approach for rapid pathogen detection, characterization, and identification. Applied R&D supports CDC/DoD collaborative efforts to operationalize Biomedical Advanced Research and Development Authority and Defense Threat Reduction Agency (DTRA) research investments and development of a systems approach for analysis of clinical samples for identification and characterization of known, emerging, and advanced biological threats. This includes genomic and proteomic technologies associated with multiplexed screening, microarrays, high-throughput sequencing, and bioinformatics analysis. This research also serves as proof of concept to address potential gaps in surveillance to detect natural or man-made changes in known agents and discover unknown/unexpected agents due to a reduced use of culture-based diagnostics.

- *Surge/follow-up capacity for clinical and non-diagnostic sample analysis:* Surge capacity is the operational capability to detect or diagnose threat agents in a large number of samples within a short time frame. The current U.S. surge capacity for emergency detection and diagnostic testing of samples generated after a potential incident relies on coordinated networking among cooperating laboratory systems. Coordination requires shared knowledge about specific laboratory sample preparation and analysis capabilities so that sample routing and results reporting can be optimized when surge capacity is required. Follow-up capacity relates to the fact that, in addition to technologies for predicting and detecting a disease outbreak, there is a need for surveillance methods specialized for use in the aftermath of an outbreak to determine the scope of the evolving threat and the level of continued risk to susceptible populations. Furthermore, novel surveillance efforts may be needed to certify that entities or areas are free of disease or to otherwise confirm exposure status for international trading partners or for other purposes.

Integrated Consortium of Laboratory Networks (ICLN): The ICLN is a DHS-chaired multiagency effort to bring together information, operations, and strategies from different laboratory systems for timely response to major incidents; participating networks include the CDC LRN, the NAHLN, the NPDN, the Food Emergency Response Network, the Environmental Response Laboratory Network, and the DoD Laboratory Network. The ICLN is a forum to share ideas, collaborate, and build relationships to support a more effective integrated response during emergencies (e.g., terrorist attacks, natural disasters, and disease outbreaks).

Capability Needs

The principal needs to improve the identification and characterization of threats include:

- Improved sensitivity, specificity, and portability of multiplexed technologies capable of identifying, with confidence, known and unknown threats in complex samples

Developing capabilities for more rapid, accurate, and comprehensive early identification and characterization of emerging or re-emerging pathogens and toxic exposures, especially for those of unknown etiology, can reduce morbidity, mortality, transmission, and consequences. Moving diagnostic capabilities to POC/PON settings will result in faster initiation of treatment, as would developing a capability to identify patients requiring treatment earlier in the progression of symptoms. When possible, such technologies should be developed so they can be sustainably adopted by healthcare practitioners in low-resource international contexts and are amenable to adaptation to high-throughput situations. Focusing investments on POC/PON tests for which there is an available treatment, or where early identification of the disease can impact patient outcomes, will facilitate adoption and increase the return on investment.

- Improved sample collection, preservation, transport, and preparation technologies and protocols

Current methods to collect, preserve, transport, and prepare clinical and non-diagnostic samples must be augmented to ensure presentation of high-quality samples for detection and diagnostic tools. This includes work to reduce the need for large sample sizes for testing, allowing for retention of as much of the original sample as possible for future evaluation.

- Improved standards for testing and evaluation of detection tools, including the development of inclusivity and exclusivity threat-agent panels and validated testing and evaluation protocols

Confidence in detection tools is hampered by inconsistent expectations about the use and performance of these tools. This inconsistency is the result of varying standards for testing and evaluation methodologies and the use of reagents/materials that are not universally recognized as reference-quality. Improving test and evaluation standards will result in better information for decision makers and higher confidence in and acceptance of results.

- Improved diagnostic technologies and access to signatures, reagents, strains, and sequence data, and an informatics and computational capabilities

To support development of diagnostic and detection platforms for known, emerging, reemerging, and unknown pathogens, there is a need for a consortium of repositories with a central catalog of signatures, reagents (including libraries of both validated reference strains and nearest neighbor strains), and taxonomic and sequence data, as well as the informatics and computational capability to support warehousing, curatorial services, querying, and modeling of disparate types of relevant data. This repository and capability will provide the means for standardized technology development, validation of technology performance, and ability to interpret results.

- Improved surveillance techniques, data sharing, and interoperability for plants, animals, and food

The ability to conduct efficient surveillance of health threats in plants, animals, and food is hampered by the lack of cost- and labor-effective methods to inspect a high percentage of these items; rapid field detection and diagnosis tools; and identification of pre-symptom or latent markers of infection or infestation. Furthermore, there are numerous databases of surveillance information in these sectors that are organized by species or industry, which contributes to a large technical gap in interoperability and minimal ability to share data from multiple disparate data streams, to inform when increased surveillance in a particular population is needed (e.g., when a spike in wildlife disease spurs increased surveillance of nearby livestock and poultry populations), or to establish a threat baseline to enable detection of emerging or re-emerging threats. It is particularly critical to improve foreign disease surveillance and data sharing capacity, and to enhance international capabilities to share critical disease surveillance data.

Research Priorities

Based on the capability needs described above and analysis of current programs, the following broad research priorities are proposed, with accompanying specific objectives:

- Development of rapid, reliable detection and diagnostic capabilities
  - Increase the speed and performance of threat detection, exposure, and disease diagnosis to support rapid and effective treatment decisions, contain disease, and mitigate the impact of a potential outbreak;
  - Move the determination of individual (asymptomatic) exposure and diagnosis of disease closer to the POC/PON setting, resulting in rapid initiation of treatment; and
  - Enhance global access to POC/PON tests.
- Development of new tools and methodologies to improve collection, preservation, transport, and preparation of clinical and non-diagnostic samples, to include maintaining sample safety, integrity, and viability/culturability
  - Ensure compatibility with nucleic acid, protein, and/or live organism characterization methods;
  - Integrate sample preparation technologies within detection or diagnostic tools, where possible, and reduce required ancillary equipment; and
  - Develop semi- to fully-automated sample collection, preservation, transportation, and preparation technologies that are compatible with current and emerging detection/diagnostic systems; are of sufficient scalability to support high throughput applications; and are deliberately developed to be sustainably adopted by healthcare practitioners in low-resource international contexts.
- Development of instrumentation and large-data-set processing capabilities to rapidly identify characteristics of known agents, rapidly detect changes in known agents, and/or to discover the existence of unknown agents from samples in clinical or environmental matrices
  - Examine characterization efforts (genotypic and phenotypic) for human, animal, and plant pathogens from high-risk areas around the world to detect emerging infectious diseases, and expand as appropriate and feasible;
  - Develop comprehensive databases linking pathogenic agents to disease outbreaks, location of origin, and other characteristics;
  - Establish a consortium of repositories of signatures, reagents, strains, and sequence data, and an informatics and computational capability for warehousing, curatorial services, querying, and modeling; and

- Develop standardized processes to conduct "what if" analyses of the environmental and health impacts of a pathogen prior to patient identification and treatment initiation.

Summary and Conclusion

Currently, the array of accurate, durable, and reliable detection, measurement of exposures, diagnostic, and characterization systems and methods is inadequate. This insufficiency can lead to early confusion as to the nature, cause, and appropriate treatment of a health threat; reliance on expensive laboratory infrastructure for analysis; and a reactive rather than proactive response to incidents. Achieving the S&T goals in this area will increase the speed and accuracy of detection, exposure assessment, and identification, characterization, and disease diagnosis; increase confidence in identifying health threats; and provide situational awareness and critical information to support decision making associated with control and prevention, to include assessment of the potential economic and health consequences of an incident and rapid and effective treatment and control decisions.

SECTION 5. INFORMATION INTEGRATION, ANALYSIS, AND SHARING

Key Research Priorities

- Development/enhancement of systems that improve near-real-time sharing of electronic health, diagnostic, and other anomalous health event data
- Development of improved mechanisms to assess data/information sources for relevancy to BSV
- Development of multilateral communication mechanisms among various levels of government, and the private sector (including healthcare providers, international partners, and others)
- Development of a national, interagency BSV data-sharing framework that integrates data/information from disparate sources

- Integration of all source data (intelligence, law enforcement, environmental, socioeconomic, and health information)
- Formalization of a means to effectively communicate uncertainty in BSV data used for decision making

Background

The overarching goal of the U.S. BSV enterprise is the ability to make informed decisions earlier, enabled by analysis of near-real-time information and integration of numerous existing efforts at varying stages of development or deployment. Data sharing and integration, as described in HSPD-21, suggests "...international connectivity where appropriate, that is predicated on state, regional, and community level capabilities and creates a networked system to allow for two-way information flow between and among Federal, state, and local government public health authorities and clinical healthcare providers." A robust global system to coordinate the integration and analysis of information does not currently exist. Improved integration and analysis of information from multilateral capabilities would provide the Nation and international community with a powerful capability for early warning of an emerging incident and situational awareness while the incident is being characterized. The architecture for this framework would be inherently complex and its operationalization will require long-term R&D efforts and international collaborations.

Current Programs

Many novel and promising BSV programs have been developed for information sharing, integration, and analysis at the Federal, state, and local levels in recent years. In 2010, the Government Accountability Office summarized more than 100 Federal data sources and systems that could contribute to a national BSV enterprise.[10] Two efforts planned or currently underway to identify these systems include an expansion of CDC's previous internal efforts to capture non-CDC information systems as part of a proposed Federal BSV Registry and an effort funded by DTRA as part of its BSV program to identify, categorize, and assess the value of potential data streams relevant to BSV systems for DoD.

Extensive efforts have been made by numerous national and regional entities to use existing human electronic health records for syndromic surveillance, exemplified nationally by DoD's Electronic Surveillance System for Early Notification of Community-based Epidemics (ESSENCE) and the CDC BioSense system, and regionally by systems such as the Pennsylvania Real-time Outbreak and Disease Surveillance system and the National Collaborative for Bio-Preparedness. These systems leverage existing health data (e.g., administrative patient discharge coding data, laboratory data, and emergency department chief complaints) from participating sources for automated, near-real-time transfer and analysis of information for early detection of anomalous health events. These types of systems have demonstrated some success for situational awareness during an event, but their ability to provide reliable and timely early warning is yet to be established.

BioSense 2.0: BioSense 2.0 is a CDC chartered, community-guided public health surveillance system that provides the capability to expand the practice of syndromic surveillance at local, state, regional, and national levels. Hosted completely in a secure internet cloud computing environment, BioSense 2.0 is capable of rapidly monitoring outbreaks and harmful health effects of hazardous agents and tracking them throughout the duration of a public health emergency utilizing hospital emergency department record data. BioSense 2.0 provides state and local health jurisdictions storage, analysis, and aggregate data sharing capabilities through a syndromic surveillance platform. By 2014, BioSense 2.0 is projected to incorporate data from 65% of state and local jurisdictions, plus data from other healthcare sources. These data will contribute timely and accurate information to the overall situation awareness of local, state, regional, and national public health.

Standards for Biosurveillance Information Exchange: HHS previously sponsored the Healthcare Information Technology Standards Panel Biosurveillance Interoperability Specification that defined standards to promote BSV information exchange among healthcare providers and public health authorities. This effort helped establish a detailed data sharing framework for electronic health record information technology systems to encourage use of systems that would provide public health information directly to a public health authority.

A number of discipline-specific and surveillance partnerships exist. For example, the NIH's Influenza Research Database is an international and domestic collaborative research effort between the Centers of Excellence for Influenza Research and Surveillance and bioinformatics/genomics research programs with a focus on integrating diverse datasets and sharing data with the influenza virus research community. The Department of State implements foreign assistance projects in the Middle East and North Africa, South and Southeast Asia, Sub-Saharan Africa, and other regions, to promote safe, secure, and sustainable bioscience capacity that improves disease diagnosis, reporting, and response. International partnerships are critical to this work, and the United Kingdom, Canada, the Netherlands, and the Republic of Korea have each provided financial contributions to help advance U.S.-led bioengagement activities abroad.

National Biosurveillance Integration System (NBIS): NBIS is a national interagency BSV integration body coordinated by the DHS National Biosurveillance Integration Center (NBIC) in accordance with a series of U.S. laws and directives (HSPD-9 and -10, Public Law 110-53 Section 1101, Food Safety Modernization Act Section 205). NBIS member agencies integrate data within their BSV domain and share this information with NBIC after the data are analyzed by their subject matter experts. NBIC, in full collaboration with the NBIS, connects, correlates, and contextualizes information across domains through the production and dissemination of its analytic products. NBIC's integrating role enhances the Federal government's ability to provide early warning and shared situational awareness.

Emerging Infections Programs (EIP): The EIP are population-based centers of excellence established through a network of state health departments collaborating with academic institutions; local health departments; public health and clinical laboratories; infection control professionals; and healthcare providers. The EIP network's unique strength and contribution lies in its ability to quickly translate surveillance and research activities into informed policy and public health practice and to maintain sufficient flexibility for emergency response as new problems arise. Surveillance efforts of the EIP activities generate reliable estimates of the incidence of certain infections and provide the foundation for a variety of epidemiologic studies to monitor prevention strategies, explore risk factors, validate diagnostics and surveillance methods, and investigate spectrum of disease.

Biosurveillance Indications and Warning Analytic Community (BIWAC): The BIWAC is a self-organized, informal BSV information sharing group with participants from multiple U.S. government organizations. The BIWAC shares BSV data via unsophisticated web interfaces and has focused on interagency collaboration and relationship building.

The DoD Joint Science and Technology Office has initiated an R&D program, called the BSV "Ecosystem" program, which aims to heavily leverage private-sector innovations in data collection and analysis that have not been previously applied to BSV. It is envisioned that data from collection and analysis systems will eventually be linked in a cloud-computing construct to serve a range of analytical customers; however, a specific architecture has yet to be developed. The DoD Joint Program Executive Office for Chemical and Biological Defense is developing a BSV communications framework termed BSV Portal (BSP) that aims to provide a single web-based environment that will facilitate collaboration, communication, and information-sharing in support of the detection, management, and mitigation of man-made and naturally occurring biological events. While the current emphasis of the BSP is focused on a subset of DoD users, it is being developed with the capability for a broader user base in the DoD and interagency space and may serve as a component of a future national BSV enterprise.

Several Federal departments and agencies and offices have invested in BSV-related R&D, including HHS (CDC, NIH), DoD, DHS, NSF, the Department of Commerce (NOAA), and USDA. Most current BSV-related investments, however, support existing data integration systems to meet the day-to-day information needs of the organization. These existing efforts could form the basis for a national-level data integration enterprise with sufficient funds, mandates, and long-term plans.

Capability Needs

- Ability to aggregate analyzed health data from different health sources, syndromic surveillance systems, and sectors to detect aberrations and discover spatial and temporal disease trends

While the potential for leveraging electronic information to augment disease surveillance is widely recognized, certain information-sharing criteria and research efforts need to be realized to advance this capability. Health data in electronic form have significant value for BSV since they provide an opportunity for more timely recognition of clinical signs in clusters of humans, animals, and plants that may provide an early indication of an emerging health incident. Effectively, appropriately, and securely sharing health event data, including parts of electronic patient records and laboratory data, has significant potential to improve national awareness of incidents that could progress to impact national security. However, a number of data-sourcing challenges exist. For example, data on human health can be collected from numerous types of patient management systems, laboratory information systems, and insurance systems, but there is a need for comprehensive terminology standardization across the spectrum of sources to ease data fusion and analysis while protecting the privacy of personal health data. Similarly, many livestock health records (domestic and foreign) are held by private industry and are not standardized from an informatics point of view, nor are they broadly accessible. Overall, there is a need for increased automated sharing and integration of electronic data from different health systems, different syndromic surveillance systems, and different health sectors.

- Ability to determine what data/information sources are relevant to BSV

The BSV community needs a systematic mechanism to categorize, evaluate, and document the expected contributions and limitations of data sources useful for local, regional, national, or international BSV efforts including early warning, early detection, and situational awareness. A few typical examples of data sources include: clinical, syndromic, diagnostic, prescription, and over-the-counter drug use; news and social media; school and work absenteeism; Internet-based early warning clearinghouses; and aggregated commercial search engine query data. Each of those broad categories can include a range of specific data sources with vastly different performance metrics due to differences in quality, completeness, or timeliness attributes, or the methodology used to analyze them. This variation provides a rich pool of potentially useful BSV data; however, it also presents challenges, as it can be difficult to assess the relative value of each source. Further, these various types of data may be subject to differing privacy laws.

- Sustained and appropriate multilateral information sharing

Producing a national BSV capability requires across-the-board collaboration of subject matter experts from different sectors (e.g., human, animal, plant, and environmental health; intelligence) at different levels of government, from the private sector, and with international partners. Active collaboration and information-sharing for BSV presents a number of challenges, especially since stakeholders have varying missions and roles, and the perceived requirements for early warning and situational awareness often necessitate novel or unconventional uses of preliminary information that cannot always be shared. Mechanisms to ensure rapid sharing (both "push" and "pull") of time-sensitive information aimed at supporting local, regional, national, or international decision- making can prove critical to achieving health and security goals. Confidentiality issues, the level of granularity to be shared among BSV systems, and actions mutually expected to result from shared information must be addressed and understood by participants in advance.

- Integration of all existing and emerging BSV efforts and cross-domain information sources into a coherent BSV enterprise

One of the biggest challenges to successful national BSV is that, to be effective, information needs to be considered simultaneously from vastly disparate domains, including health, law enforcement, intelligence, environmental monitoring, remote sensing, international partners, and many others. Each domain has its own culture, investigative methodology, and tolerance for the timeliness and completeness of information necessary to make decisions and initiate response actions. Additionally, there are dozens and possibly hundreds of BSV initiatives and pilot projects that have been started at local, state, regional, and national levels. Without a universal system for integration of multiple, disparate data sources relevant to BSV, the synergistic value of bringing these data together will not be attained.

- Standardized methods for determining the uncertainty in BSV data and clearly communicating the limits of the data and analytical techniques

For information to be actionable, some assessment and communication of its validity and accuracy is needed. BSV data present many analysis challenges because they can be inconsistently collected, reported, and analyzed; may contain collection and other types of data biases; can be derived from many disparate or incongruent sources; and may have gaps in temporal and spatial coverage. Each of these factors can add uncertainty to any analysis. In addition, local contextual knowledge is often needed to interpret the significance of any statistical deviation. These influences may or may not be known to the data owners and, as the data are analyzed by others, re-purposed, or otherwise reach a broader audience, the nuances related to specific data uncertainties may not be consistently and appropriately communicated. As a result, human expertise, which may be enhanced by technology, is key to a successful BSV enterprise. Research related to uncertainty quantification and communication is required to ensure decision makers are fully aware of the strengths and weakness of inferences that may be made as a result of BSV data analysis.

Research Priorities

Based on the capability needs described above and analysis of current programs, the following broad research priorities are proposed, with accompanying specific objectives:

- Development/enhancement of systems that improve near real-time sharing of electronic health, diagnostic, and other anomalous health event data
  - Develop systems for human, animal, and plant electronic health data with capacity for standardizing data elements to allow for potential interoperability of systems and data integration, including with international partners as appropriate;
  - Define a common "near-real-time" requirement for early incident detection, given the varying requirements among sectors; and
  - Develop standards to ensure secure, automated data transmission with rule-based sharing and role-based authentication.
- Development of improved mechanisms to assess data/information sources for relevancy to BSV
  - Continue efforts to define and establish mechanisms to assess data/information sources, particularly through coordination of DoD, HHS, and DHS efforts and with the rest of Federal interagency;
  - Develop and use metrics for each category of data source (e.g., sensitivity, specificity, timeliness) to assess the utility of tools, training programs, and strategies employed to support national and global BSV efforts; and
  - Establish a process and test data sets for calibration and system performance comparisons to assess whether a source is primarily beneficial for earliest possible detection, situational awareness, impact forecasting, and/or response efforts.
- Development of multilateral communication mechanisms among various levels of government and the private sector (including healthcare providers, international partners, and others) to enable timely decision making at all levels

- Develop a community-endorsed and championed primary BSV Common Operating Picture, leveraging existing capabilities and lessons learned, to collect and share information at a national level and display a level of BSV information, including analyst insight, necessary to inform operational decision-makers across the government;
- Evaluate ways to establish enduring, analyst-focused trust relationships across sectors and domains—and among international partners, organizations, and nongovernmental organizations—to facilitate a multi-institutional culture of information sharing; and
- Establish mechanisms to securely transfer finished or unfinished information at different levels (e.g., open-source, sensitive, classified) among stakeholders and decision makers to enhance integration and usability.

• Development of a national, interagency BSV data-sharing framework that integrates data/information from disparate sources to enable early warning and early detection of incidents and situational awareness during an incident
  - Integrate various existing and emerging BSV efforts and cross-domain information sources into a coherent BSV enterprise. This path forward may require a "system-ofsystems" approach that capitalizes on successes and capabilities of the many existing systems by linking them in a new national BSV framework that does not currently exist; and
  - Develop a viable approach for state and local authorities to access a national, interagency BSV data-sharing framework, as well as ways to collect their data.

• Integration of all source data (intelligence, law enforcement, environmental, socioeconomic, and health information) to enhance the detection of a disease event and facilitate warning and forecasting of impact
  - Continue development of automation tools that allow efficient knowledge discovery through exploitation of existing large and massive data sets, particularly unstructured massive information stores such as PubMed, the National Center for Biotechnology Information, and other National Library of Medicine resources; as well as social media; online engine searches; and traditional media reporting; and

  - Establish an interagency BSV information technology development, information management, and knowledge generation coordination initiative.
- Formalization of a means to effectively communicate uncertainty in BSV data used for decision making
  - Develop standardized methods for determining the uncertainty in BSV data and clearly communicating the limits of the data and analytical techniques.

Summary and Conclusion

A major challenge to successful national BSV is that information must be considered simultaneously from vastly disparate domains, including health, law enforcement, intelligence, and international partners. Sharing of this information is limited, due to real or perceived confidentiality and other issues, and is often not possible.

Integration of multilateral capabilities will enable strengths and resources to be leveraged, providing a powerful capability for early warning and situational awareness. Successful implementation of a national BSV enterprise will support a more comprehensive national information sharing capability to save lives and reduce illness.

Conclusion

Meeting the challenge of establishing the national BSV enterprise called for in the *Strategy* will be difficult, but is not insurmountable. Progress has already been made and current programs and technologies are making strides toward meeting the *Strategy's* goals. Continuing this progress will require focusing investments and coordinating efforts across the Federal Government on enabling S&T, with participation from academia, industry, and international partners.

Investing in the goals identified in this *Roadmap* will increase the speed and accuracy of disease detection, identification, characterization, and information sharing and support decision making associated with rapid disease control, prevention, and treatment.

APPENDIX A. SECTION 4 GLOSSARY

Characterization: Determination of one or more physical, chemical, or biological properties, characteristics, and/or identities of a material and/or biological entity. For example, characterization tests could include determination of agent strain, viability, or transmissibility.

Clinical laboratory: Facility for the biological, microbiological, serological, chemical, immunohematological, biophysical, cytological, pathological, or other examination of clinical samples (see below) to provide information for the diagnosis, prevention, or treatment of any disease or impairment; or of assessing the health of humans, animals, or plants.

Clinical sample: A discrete, unaltered portion taken from a human, animal, or plant for the purpose of examination, study, or analysis to inform diagnosis and treatment.

Detection: Initial determination of the presence or absence of an agent or target in a given matrix; for example, detection of a nucleic acid signature of a known threat in physiological tissues, soil samples, or in an aerosol monitoring system.

Diagnosis: Interpretation of diagnostic (see below) result(s) to inform treatment and control options.

Diagnostic: Reagents, instruments, and systems intended for use in diagnosis of disease or other conditions, including a determination of the state of health, in order to cure, mitigate, treat, or prevent disease or its sequelae.

Non-diagnostic sample: Any sample from the environment, food, plants, animals, or humans analyzed for surveillance or detection purposes but not used in a treatment decision.

Identification: Determination of specific details about an agent present in a given environment, matrix, or clinical sample. For example, identification includes strain classification coupled with expressed plasmids and mapped antibiotic resistance genes.

Laboratory: Facility for the biological, microbiological, serological, chemical, immunohematological, biophysical, cytological, pathological, or other examination of non-diagnostic samples.

Point-of-need (PON): Analysis performed by non-medical personnel in close proximity to sample collection point. For example, field analysis of white powders, use of home pregnancy tests, or surveillance for pathogens and pests at ports of entry.

Point-of-care (POC): Analysis of pathogen presence and/or exposure in the health care environment immediately surrounding a patient. Examples include bed-side tests in a medical unit, ambulance, or mobile transport vehicle, or a physician's office.

Signature: Unique identifying component of a threat (e.g., for biological samples; nucleic acids, proteins, etc.).

APPENDIX B. BST WG SUB-WORKING GROUP MEMBERSHIP

Aberration Detection

Taha Kass-Hout – CO-CHAIR
Department of Health and Human Services Food and Drug Administration

Russ Bulluck
Department of Agriculture
Animal and Plant Health Inspection Service

Geoff Scott
Department of Commerce
National Oceanic and Atmospheric Administration

Chris Kiley
Department of Defense
Defense Threat Reduction Agency Joint Science and Technology Office

Seth Foldy
Department of Health and Human Services Centers for Disease Control and Prevention

Nancy Jones
Department of Health and Human Services
National Institutes of Health

Samantha Gibbs
Department of the Interior U.S. Fish and Wildlife Center

Jonathan Sleeman
Department of the Interior U.S. Geological Survey National Wildlife Health Center

Charles Liarakos – CO-CHAIR National Science Foundation

Randall Levings
Department of Agriculture
Animal and Plant Health Inspection Service

Julie Pavlin
Department of Defense
Armed Forces Health Surveillance Center

Scott Remine
Department of Defense
Joint Program Executive Office for Chemical and Biological Defense

Carole Heilman
Department of Health and Human Services National Institutes of Health

Patricia Strickler-Dinglasan
Department of Health and Human Services National Institutes of Health

Adam Kramer
Department of the Interior National Park Service

Risk Anticipation

Geoff Scott – CO-CHAIR Department of Commerce
National Oceanic and Atmospheric Administration

Adia Bogossian
Department of Agriculture
Animal and Plant Health Inspection Service

Andrew Wilds
Department of Agriculture
Animal and Plant Health Inspection Service

Felix Kogan
Department of Commerce
National Oceanic and Atmospheric Administration

Madeline Thomson
Department of Commerce
National Oceanic and Atmospheric Administration

Christopher Perdue
Department of Defense
Armed Forces Health Surveillance Center

Erica Carroll
Department of Defense
Defense Threat Reduction Agency Joint Science and Technology Office

Dylan George
Department of Defense
National Center for Medical Intelligence

Carole Heilman
Department of Health and Human Services National Institutes of Health

Patricia Strickler-Dinglasan
Department of Health and Human Services National Institutes of Health

Ed Espinoza
Department of the Interior U.S. Fish and Wildlife Service

Debra Gulick
Department of State

Helen Cui
Los Alamos National Laboratory

Glenn Dowling – CO-CHAIR Department of Defense
National Center for Medical Intelligence

Ron Sequeira
Department of Agriculture
Animal and Plant Health Inspection Service

Jan Carson
Department of Commerce
National Oceanic and Atmospheric Administration

Chris Miller
Department of Commerce
National Oceanic and Atmospheric Administration

Thiaw Wassila
Department of Commerce
National Oceanic and Atmospheric Administration

Roger Breeze
Department of Defense
Defense Threat Reduction Agency Joint Science and Technology Office

Bob Huffman
Department of Defense
Joint Program Executive Office for Chemical and Biological Defense

Nathaniel Hupert
Department of Health and Human Services Centers for Disease Control and Prevention

Nancy Jones
Department of Health and Human Services National Institutes of Health

David Wong
Department of the Interior National Park Service

John Pearce
Department of the Interior U.S. Geological Survey

Gary Resnick
Los Alamos National Laboratory

Threat Identification and Characterization

Anne Hultgren – CO-CHAIR Department of Homeland Security Science and Technology Directorate

Robert von Tersch – CO-CHAIR
Office of the Assistant Secretary of Defense for Nuclear, Chemical, and Biological Defense Programs

Randall Levings
Department of Agriculture
Animal and Plant Health Inspection Service

Mike McIntosh
Department of Agriculture
Animal and Plant Health Inspection Service

Luther Lindler
Department of Defense
Armed Forces Health Surveillance Center

Scott Remine
Department of Defense
Joint Program Executive Office for Chemical and Biological Defense

Philip LoBue
Department of Health and Human Services Centers for Disease Control and Prevention

Patricia Strickler-Dinglasan
Department of Health and Human Services National Institutes of Health

Nancy Jones
Department of Health and Human Services National Institutes of Health

Sara Newman
Department of the Interior National Park Service

Sanjiv Shah
Environmental Protection Agency

Clay Holloway – CO-CHAIR
Department of Defense
Office of the Assistant Secretary of Defense for Nuclear, Chemical, and Biological Defense Programs

Laurene Levy
Department of Agriculture
Animal and Plant Health Inspection Service

Scott Cross
Department of Commerce
National Oceanic and Atmospheric Administration

Eric Van Gieson
Department of Defense
Defense Threat Reduction Agency Joint Science and Technology Office

Richard Kellogg
Department of Health and Human Services Centers for Disease Control and Prevention

Sally Hojvat
Department of Health and Human Services Food and Drug Administration

Carole Heilman
Department of Health and Human Services National Institutes of Health

Jessica Appler
Department of Homeland Security Science and Technology Directorate

Jonathan Sleeman
Department of the Interior U.S. Geological Survey
National Wildlife Health Center

Information Integration, Analysis, and Sharing

Tom Bates – CO-CHAIR
Lawrence Livermore National Laboratory

Shantini Gamage – CO-CHAIR Department of Veterans Affairs

Lynn Tracey
Department of Agriculture
Animal and Plant Health Inspection Service

Scott Cross
Department of Commerce
National Oceanic and Atmospheric Administration

John Hannan
Department of Defense
Defense Threat Reduction Agency Joint Science and Technology Office

Deena Disraelly
Department of Defense
Joint Program Executive Office for Chemical and Biological Defense

Jennifer Olson
Department of Health and Human Services
Biomedical Advanced Research and Development Authority

Carole Heilman
Department of Health and Human Services
National Institutes of Health

Patricia Strickler-Dinglasan
Department of Health and Human Services National Institutes of Health

Jessica Appler
Department of Homeland Security Science and Technology Directorate

John Quinn
Department of Veterans Affairs

Molly Brown
National Aeronautics and Space Administration

Chris Decker
Office of the Director of National Intelligence

Gary Roselle – CO-CHAIR Department of Veterans Affairs

Rick Zink
Department of Agriculture
Animal and Plant Health Inspection Service

Rohit Chitale
Department of Defense
Armed Forces Health Surveillance Center

Nancy Nurthen
Department of Defense
Defense Threat Reduction Agency
Joint Science and Technology Office

Karen House
Department of Defense
Joint Program Executive Office for Chemical and Biological Defense

William Morrill
Department of Health and Human Services
Centers for Disease Control and Prevention

Nancy Jones
Department of Health and Human Services
National Institutes of Health

Teresa Quitugua
Department of Homeland Security Office of Health Affairs

Charlie Stroup
Department of Veterans Affairs

Ray Arthur
Department of Health and Human Services
Centers for Disease Control and Prevention

Clyde Manning
Office of the Director of National Intelligence

End Notes

[1] Biosurveillance is the process of gathering, integrating, interpreting, and communicating essential information related to all-hazards threats or disease activity affecting human, animal, or plant health to achieve early detection and warning, contribute to overall situational awareness of the health aspects of an incident, and to enable better decision making at all levels.

[2] S&T to enable improved mitigation, response, and recovery is described in a separate S&T Roadmap in production by the Biological Response and Recovery Working Group. Development, efficacy, and recommended use of post-exposure prophylaxis and/or other medical countermeasures are addressed in the 2012 HHS Public Health Emergency Medical Countermeasures Enterprise Strategy and Implementation Plan.

[3] http://commonfund.nih.gov/hmp/

[4] http://www.aphis.usda.gov/animal_health/nahms/

[5] http://www.fic.nih.gov/programs/Pages/ecology-infectious-diseases.aspx

[6] http://www.fic.nih.gov/about/staff/pages/epidemiology-population.aspx

[7] http://eros.usgs.gov/

[8] http://www.aphis.usda.gov/animal_health/nahln/

[9] http://www.npdn.org/

[10] http://www.gao.gov/assets/310/306362.pdf

In: National Biosurveillance Strategy ... ISBN: 978-1-62948-994-0
Editor: Amanda Wendell

Chapter 3

BIOLOGICAL RESPONSE AND RECOVERY SCIENCE AND TECHNOLOGY ROADMAP*

Biological Response and Recovery Science and Technology Working Group

October 25, 2013

Dear Colleague:

I am pleased to transmit the enclosed *Biological Response and Recovery Science and Technology Roadmap*, produced under the auspices of the Committee on Homeland and National Security of the National Science and Technology Council (NSTC).

The report categorizes key scientific knowledge gaps, identifies technology solutions, and prioritizes research areas to enable government, at all levels, to make decisions more effectively during the response to and recovery from a biological incident—whether naturally occurring or intentional.

A catastrophic biological incident could threaten the Nation's human, animal, plant, environmental, and economic health, as well as America's national security. Such an event would demand a rapid and effective response in order to: (1) minimize loss of life and other adverse consequences

* This report was released by the Executive Office of the President, National Science and Technology Council, Office of Science and Technology Policy, October 2013.

associated with the incident and (2) thwart ongoing threats and follow-on attacks in the case of suspected criminal activity or terrorism.

This report builds on the *National Biosurveillance Science and Technology Roadmap*, which was released by the NSTC in June 2013, and focused on how to better monitor and track events that could lead to a biological incident.

The new roadmap sets near-term objectives and long-term goals for coordinated research and development (R&D) activities among Federal agencies to strengthen evidence-based decision making and response and recovery efforts during a biological incident or after one occurs.

Thank you for your interest in Federal R&D efforts to ensure the United States is fully able to mount an effective response to and recovery from a catastrophic biological incident. This work is critically important to the health, safety, and security of our Nation.

Sincerely,

John P. Holdren
Assistant to the President for Science and Technology Director,
Office of Science & Technology Policy

ABBREVIATIONS AND ACRONYMS LIST

AAP	American Academy of Pediatrics
ASDWA	Association of State Drinking Water Administrators
ASPR	Assistant Secretary for Preparedness and Response
ASTHO	Association of State and Territorial Health Officials
BDRD	Biological Defense Research and Development
BOTE	Bio-response Operational Testing and Evaluation
BRRST WG	Biological Response and Recovery Science and Technology Working Group
CBRN	Chemical, Biological, Radiological, and Nuclear
CDC	Centers for Disease Control and Prevention
CHNS	Committee on Homeland and National Security
DeconST	Decontamination Decision Support Tool
DFoS	Decontamination Family of Systems
DHS	Department of Homeland Security
DOD	Department of Defense

DTRA	Defense Threat Reduction Agency
EM2P	Emergency Management Modernization Program
EPA	Environmental Protection Agency
FBI	Federal Bureau of Investigation
FDA	Food and Drug Administration
FERN	Food Emergency Response Network
GIS	Geographic Information Systems
HHS	Health and Human Services
HRDS	Human Remains Decontamination System
ICLN	Integrated Consortium of Laboratory Networks
JPEO-CBD	Joint Program Executive Office for Chemical and Biological Defense
LRN	Laboratory Response Network
MCM	Medical Countermeasures
NACCHO	National Association of County and City Health Officials
NASGLP	North American Soil Geochemical Landscapes Project
NEHA	National Environmental Health Association
NHSRC	National Homeland Security Research Center
NSTC	National Science and Technology Council
OSTP	Office of Science and Technology Policy
PHEMCE	Public Health Emergency Medical Countermeasures Enterprise
RV-PCR	Rapid Viability Polymerase Chain Reaction
SOP	Standard Operating Procedure
SPORE	Scientific Program on Reaerosolization and Exposure
S&T	Science and technology
STEM	Science, Technology, Engineering, and Math
TaCBRD	Transatlantic Collaborative Biological Resiliency Demonstration
USDA	United States Department of Agriculture
USGS	U.S. Geological Survey
Vet-LIRN	Veterinary Laboratory Investigation and Response Network
WARRP	Wide Area Recovery and Resiliency Program
WG	Working Group

EXECUTIVE SUMMARY

A catastrophic biological incident could threaten the Nation's human, animal, plant, environmental, and economic health, as well as America's national security. Such an event would demand a quick and effective response in order to minimize loss of life and other adverse consequences and, in the case of suspected criminal activity or terrorism, to thwart ongoing activity and prevent follow-on attacks. But response and recovery from a catastrophic biological incident is not a simple, formulaic process. Rather, it is a continuous process of data and information collection, evidence-based review, and decision making, all leading to an informed and constantly evolving series of critical and coordinated actions. Moreover, the response and recovery process involves the integration and coordination of data and capabilities from many different sectors, including public health, law enforcement, waste management, infrastructure management, and transportation. Strategic science and technology (S&T) investments are essential to provide the information that can support evidence-based operational decisions and strengthen response-and-recovery efforts. *This report categorizes key scientific knowledge gaps, identifies technology solutions to these gaps, and prioritizes research areas that will enable government at all levels to make decisions more effectively during the response to, and recovery from, biological incidents.*

The prioritized, near-term objectives and broader, long-term goals presented in this report constitute a roadmap for use by Federal departments and agencies to coordinate their research and development (R&D) activities. The primary near-term objectives whose timely achievement this roadmap aims to facilitate are:

- Establish the location(s) of the confirmed biological agent in the environment;
- Develop reliable estimates of risk of exposure for a multitude of environments, matrices, and conditions associated with wide-area release scenarios;
- Develop reliable estimates of risk to humans, animals, and plants through various exposure and transmission routes;
- Develop risk reduction strategies, including decontamination, waste management, contaminant control, and reaerosolization control, for a variety of biological threats and scenarios;

- Evaluate population infection prevention measures (e.g., quarantine, isolation, and social distancing) used to reduce incident impact and develop a strong scientific basis for recommending these measures; and
- Use risk communication research to guide development of appropriate messages and dissemination means to stakeholders, including decision makers, first responders, the public, and the media.

Coordination of R&D agendas among Federal departments and agencies will reduce duplication of effort and enhance efficiencies as the Nation enhances its capacity to prevent, protect against, mitigate, respond to, and recover from catastrophic biological incidents.

SECTION 1. INTRODUCTION

> "Just as we step up our ability to prevent an attack, we must also bolster our capacity to protect against — and respond to — the threats that may come. When it comes to bioterror, this can mean the difference between a contained incident and a catastrophe. That's why we need to invest in new vaccines, to reduce the risk posed by those who would use disease as a weapon. That's why we must develop the technology to detect attacks and to trace them to their origin, so that we can react in a timely fashion. And to care for our citizens who are infected, we must provide our public health system across the country with the surge capacity to confront a crisis. Making these changes will do more than help us tackle bioterror — it will create new jobs, support a healthier population, and improve America's capability to respond to any major disaster."
>
> —President Barack Obama (July 16, 2008)

Background

A biological incident may be caused by a naturally-occurring outbreak with a human, plant, or animal pathogen, such as the 2009 H1N1 pandemic; the deliberate dissemination of pathogens, such as the 2001 U.S. anthrax attacks; or the accidental release of biological agents, such as the 2007 release of foot-and-mouth disease virus from a laboratory in the United Kingdom.

Such events can have devastating impacts on public, animal, or plant health, the economy, critical infrastructure, military readiness, and public confidence. Effective response to and recovery from a catastrophic biological incident can mitigate all those risks, but will depend upon rapid, sound decisions being made by response personnel and government officials.

In working toward that goal, the Secretaries of the U.S. Departments of Health and Human Services, Agriculture, Interior, Defense, Commerce, and Homeland Security, as well as the Administrator of the Environmental Protection Agency and the U.S. Attorney General, with the support of other Federal partners, are guided by the National Response Framework[1] and specific Presidential Policy Directive-8[2] frameworks to support local authorities in making critical decisions to enable effective response and recovery from a biological incident.

To ensure the United States is fully able to mount an effective response to and recovery from a catastrophic biological incident, the Subcommittee on Biological Defense Research and Development (BDRD), under the Committee on Homeland and National Security of the National Science and Technology Council, chartered the Biological Response and Recovery Science and Technology (BRRST) Working Group (WG) to assess biological incident response and recovery capabilities and recommend a way forward towards addressing scientific knowledge or technological gaps to improve decision making.

Overview of the Response and Recovery Process

Response to and recovery from a catastrophic biological incident requires a continuous and coordinated process of data and information collection, review, and decision making that results in a series of critical and coordinated actions (Figure 1). Science and technology (S&T) provide the knowledge and tools for effective response and recovery operations. Throughout the response and recovery process, decisions depend on what is known about the agent's transmission dynamics, chain of infection, and other data that may change or evolve as the incident matures and the response unfolds. Response includes those capabilities necessary to save and sustain lives; mitigate human, environmental, plant, and animal health impacts; stabilize the incident; protect property and the environment; meet basic human needs after an incident has occurred; and, in the case of suspected Federal crimes or terrorism, thwart continued activity and prevent follow-on attacks. The ability to make sound decisions in the first minutes, hours, and days following an incident can make a significant difference in lives saved, extent of the spread of disease, and duration of the overall recovery.

Key elements of an effective biological response and recovery are described in the 2009 Draft document, "Planning Guidance for Recovery Following Biological Incidents"[3]. Briefly, the first phase of activities includes detection and confirmation of a biological incident, followed by notification/early warning and first response. Decisions to begin notification procedures and initiate communications regarding an incident require confidence in the identification and confirmation process, as well as guidance on operational coordination and communications strategies for disseminating information about the incident to appropriate authorities and the public.

Notification/early warning procedures provide situational awareness by confirming for proper authorities and the public that a biological incident has occurred. First response is a series of decisions and actions immediately following notification that aim to effectively control, contain, investigate, and mitigate the effects of a biological incident. First response may include initial site containment, environmental sampling and analysis, and public health activities such as treatment of potentially exposed persons and industry engagement. It may also include a law enforcement response, tactical and technical operations, designation of crime scenes, and related activities.

Restoring basic services and supporting the transition to recovery are also critical elements of a timely response to a biological incident. Restoration and recovery encompass the process of returning a community to a state of normality after a disastrous biological incident and requires, among other elements, ongoing characterization of the environment to determine health risks. Efforts to support restoration and, as appropriate, re-occupancy following a biological incident include elements of communicating the risk associated with returning an area to normal use and how best to reduce risk of infection or exposure through remediation processes. Federal, state, or local public health officials, government departments and agencies, and/or property owners (depending on site-specific jurisdictional authorities) make final decisions on clearance.

Environmental stability of biological pathogens varies greatly among various organisms, and restoration, clearance, and re-occupancy can range from relatively uncomplicated processes to large-scale decontamination processes.

Capability Gaps

While substantial progress has been made to prevent, detect, respond to, and recover from natural, accidental, and intentional outbreaks, additional focused S&T efforts that leverage investments by Federal departments and agencies and integrate knowledge from advancements in the biological sciences are required to fill critical capability gaps that currently hamper decision makers. Among the numerous factors that can undermine an effective response to an incident are the lag between the incident occurrence and its detection and/or confirmation; lack of understanding of agent spread, transport, and persistence in the environment; lack of clarity about the actual impacted or contaminated area; and uncertainty due to technical limitations and gaps in knowledge and information to drive decision making. Additionally, biological contamination with certain agents presents unique remediation challenges because of the ability of the agent to infect and replicate in a host and/or persist or propagate and thrive in the environment. For example, periodic natural outbreaks of anthrax in animals throughout the world demonstrate the persistence and transport of the organism in the environment. Likewise, seasonal outbreaks of influenza show a persistence of the causative virus in human and animal reservoirs. Biological structure, metabolic characteristics, and natural history of biological agents in conjunction with the physical and climatic conditions in the surrounding environment define the survival rate and hence the fate of the agent outside of its host or hosts. Changing conditions affect the presence and persistence of an agent in the environment, which influences the risk posed and drives the choice of risk-reduction strategies. Therefore, response and recovery processes, including a variety of risk-reduction strategies, are dependent upon a comprehensive understanding of the agent and the human and environmental contexts in which it exists.

Roadmap Development Process

To define the path forward outlined in this *Roadmap*, the BRRST WG developed a working document that described the decisions that first responders or government officials would need to make following a biological incident, what questions the decision maker might ask, and, of those questions, which could be addressed with scientific information or technological capabilities. While the framework established in the draft "Planning Guidance for Recovery Following Biological Incidents" focuses only on remediation/cleanup recovery operations after contamination with *Bacillus anthracis*, the causative agent of anthrax, that framework serves as a starting point for describing the decisions that need to be made in response to biological incidents in general. Based on the phases and activities outlined in that framework, the BRRST WG developed a list of major (high-impact) decisions that would need to be made during each phase of response and recovery (Figure 1). (The decisions and activities presented in Figure 1 are nominally categorized according to their relative timing within the response and recovery timeline but the timing of their implementation can vary—e.g., some limited decontamination operations and waste generation may begin with the first response activities and implementing public messaging generally occurs throughout the entire process).

The resultant working document was used to guide discussions and to collect Federal department and agency information on current and planned programmatic activity with the potential to address the questions answerable by S&T. Review of submitted information on Federal activities drove the development of S&T capability goals and objectives. Those goals and objectives constitute the heart of this Roadmap and comprise a guide for future Federal, academic, and industrial S&T efforts and for international collaborations. Sidebars highlighting some successful S&T programs have been included in this report as well, to demonstrate where current programs are working to address some of the gaps identified and where expansion of ongoing activities would be beneficial. While the intent was to create a Roadmap that applies to a variety of biological agents, it should be noted that many components and highlighted programs in this Roadmap apply in particular to agents that pose the difficult challenge of persisting in the environment (e.g., Bacillus anthracis).

Purpose and Scope

The strategic goals and objectives presented in this *Roadmap* aim to focus Federal S&T efforts with the goal of enhancing operational decisions at various phases of the response and recovery process. This *Roadmap* complements, but does not duplicate, ongoing S&T collaboration in the area of Biosurveillance and Medical Countermeasures (MCM) that address S&T needs for protection against the occurrence of a biological incident; initial detection, diagnosis, or confirmation of a biological agent; prediction of the occurrence of or forecasting the impact of a biological incident or the development and use of MCM.

Response and Recovery					
Crisis Management		Consequence Management			
Notification	First Response	Remediation/Cleanup			Restoration/ Re-occupancy
		Characterization	Decontamination	Clearance	
Initiate first response activities, including notification of proper authorities Develop a public-engagement campaign Evaluate Threat Credibility	Operational Coordination Law enforcement, intelligence, and investigative response When and how to distribute medical countermeasures Recommend staying-in-place or evacuation Recommend quarantine/isolation/ social distancing Implement transportation restrictions Provide safety and health guidance and protections to impacted first responders and citizens Issue guidance on personal hygiene or decontamination Provide support for mass casualty Establish mass medical treatment facilities Implement modified standards of care	Develop/ implement strategies for characterization in facilities and the outdoors Implement strategies and procedures to identify, stabilize, and maintain infrastructure and property Determine requirements and methods to protect natural and cultural resources Implement strategies and means to contain and mitigate the spread of contamination and eliminate sources of further distribution (e.g., insecticides for flies)	Decontaminate outdoor areas and/or buildings Decontaminate wide areas Implement required capabilities for sustained environmental decontamination operations Implement decontamination waste handling requirements Decontaminate critical infrastructure	Provide guidance for determination of effectiveness of decontamination	Provide guidance for re-occupancy and reuse criteria and goals Provide guidance for controls to implement, reduce, mitigate any potential exposures or future incidents after re-occupancy Implement public messaging to instill confidence in the public and workforce that re-occupancy is safe Implement measures to retain, maintain and improve the economic vitality of a region Implement long term health treatment, intervention and surveillance strategy

Figure 1. Key Response and Recovery Decisions.

SECTION 2. CAPABILITY GOALS TO SUPPORT CRITICAL RESPONSE AND RECOVERY DECISIONS

This Roadmap presents the S&T needs to support the following critical operational decisions that may be required at various phases of response and recovery following confirmation of a biological incident:

- Develop/implement strategies for characterization both indoors and outdoors
- Determine when and how to distribute medical countermeasures[4]
- Recommend staying-in-place or evacuation
- Recommend quarantine, isolation, or social distancing
- Implement transportation restrictions
- Provide safety and health guidance and protections to impacted first responders and the public
- Implement strategies and methods to contain and mitigate the spread of contamination
- Provide guidance for determination of effectiveness of decontamination
- Provide guidance for re-occupancy and reuse criteria and goals
- Decontaminate outdoor areas and/or buildings
- Implement decontamination and waste handling requirements
- Provide guidance for controls to implement, reduce, mitigate any potential exposures or future incidents after re-occupancy

The high-level goals below describe relative end-states that will enable decision making, while the objectives and accompanying sub-objectives identify scientific knowledge and technological needs to achieve those end states.

Goal 1: Characterize the extent of the incident to reduce exposure and save lives.

Biological incidents must be adequately characterized in order to enable effective decision making. Validated methods for environmental analysis can inform decision makers of the extent of an incident and guide actions such as recommending evacuation or staying-in-place or determining the extent to which MCMs are needed. This capacity requires high-throughput methods to support surge capacity for wide-area and large-scale incident characterization; coordinated sample-collection and analysis capability to support multiple agencies during response and recovery operations; and real-time modeling tools to support biosurveillance operations, including a capacity to incorporate post-incident characterization data to identify potentially contaminated areas and guide response and recovery operations.

Integrated Consortium of Laboratory Networks (ICLN)

The ICLN is a multiagency effort chaired by the Department of Homeland Security (DHS) to bring together information, operations, and strategies from different laboratory systems for timely response to major incidents; participating networks include the Centers for Disease Control and Prevention's (CDC) Laboratory Response Network (LRN), the National Animal Health Laboratory Network (NAHLN), the National Plant Diagnostic Network, the Food Emergency Response Network (FERN), the Environmental Response Laboratory Network, the Veterinary Laboratory Investigation and Response Network (Vet-LIRN) and the Department of Defense (DOD) Laboratory Network. The ICLN is a forum to facilitate communication and collaboration to build relationships and tools to support a more effective integrated laboratory response during emergencies (e.g., terrorist attacks, natural disasters, and disease outbreaks). ICLN activities include work to harmonize rapid-screening protocols for a pathogen outbreak, develop assay-sharing and testing reciprocity policies, enable transfer of laboratory data between networks, promote network compatibility/interoperability, and develop information-sharing policies for surge-capacity demands.

Rapid Viability Polymerase Chain Reaction (RV-PCR)

The RV-PCR method was developed for detection of live *B. anthracis* spores in surface wipe, air filter, and water samples. It has been optimized to achieve a limit of detection of 10 to 99 *B. anthracis* spores per sample. The method is most useful during the recovery phase of the response because it allows for rapid and high-throughput sample analysis to determine presence or absence of viable (live) *B. anthracis* spores (in the presence of a large number of inactivated/dead spores). The method supports rapid response and recovery following a *B. anthracis* contamination incident. Products from the research efforts can be accessed at www.epa.gov/sam/BAPROTOCOL.pdf and www.epa.gov/sam/.

Protocol for Detection of *B. anthracis* in Environmental Samples During the Remediation Phase of an Anthrax Event

This step-by-step protocol (http://cfpub.epa.gov/si/si_public_record_report.cfm?dirEntryId=247752) was developed for EPA's Environmental Response Laboratory Network and Water Laboratory Alliance to support remediation decisions. The broad promulgation of this protocol has effectively increased laboratory capacity to analyze anthrax samples during a wide-area event. The protocol includes adaptation of many procedures of the CDC's LRN protocols which will lead to increased confidence in sample analyses.

Objectives to achieve characterization of the extent of the incident and to reduce exposure include:

1. Establish the location(s) of the confirmed biological agent in the environment.
   a) Identify and verify performance for environmental sample collection, preservation, transport, preparation technologies, and protocols for high priority agents that can be rapidly adapted for a large-scale incident;
   b) Establish appropriate test and evaluation capability for rapid environmental contamination detection technologies to ensure reliable and consistent performance across the response and recovery operations; and

c) Develop integrated sampling strategies, guidance, and training to support capabilities for environmental sampling and analysis.

2. Integrate incident characterization data into biosurveillance situational awareness modeling tools.
   a) Develop protocols and technologies to rapidly assess agent critical characteristics, spread potential (including secondary aerosolization), and environmental persistence;
   b) Develop capability to integrate rapid field-to-lab and lab-to-field data and results interpretation into biosurveillance modeling tools; and
   c) c. Ensure that biosurveillance situational awareness modeling tools provide capability to rapidly forecast incident physical perimeters, estimate risk of environmental exposure, translate and integrate analytical, intelligence, and clinical surveillance data.

Goal 2: Effectively communicate to reduce the impacts of a biological incident.

Effective response and recovery operations require Federal, state, and local leaders to have the tools and messages they need to rapidly and effectively communicate with each other, the public, the media, and the response community during a biological incident. Effective communication is critical to quickly and accurately convey information that can mitigate the consequences of an incident; provide consistent guidance to the public on what immediate actions they should take to protect themselves; and provide guidance to the public as to when it is safe to return to affected areas. Because information travels quickly through social media, leaders at all levels of government need to be aware of the challenges and opportunities that the modern media landscape may present during an incident. For example, quick communication of an incident through social media might require rapid, high-consequence decisions (such as ordering evacuations, quarantines, release of MCM stockpiles) early on and in the face of high uncertainty. However, effective risk communication plans using social media and traditional media (e.g., radio and TV) can be prepared before an incident, pulled “off the shelf,” adapted to fit the specifics of an incident, and used to quickly disseminate life-saving information to the public. This information can be tailored and delivered to targeted audiences based on their locations and circumstances. Additionally, decision makers can use social media to obtain feedback from people in the affected areas, which may be useful to assess and improve response and recovery operations.

Risk communication during an incident requires previously verified communication systems, interoperability, and focus-group or other testing of message content. Questions arise around how best to distribute information and what types of information to distribute, and how that information will be received. Building a foundation in the social science of effective communication is critical to creating effective media communication mechanisms and leveraging existing social media networks. Regardless of the type of information, science-based knowledge products and improved technologies to assess consequences and impacts of interventions will support the implementation of informed, coordinated, public messaging campaigns.

Generation of Risk Communication Best Practices

The EPA, in conjunction with county governments and academic institutions, is conducting multi-year studies of risk-communication best practices and is eliciting stakeholder and public input to determine risk communication needs and test pre-scripted messages. To date, the best practices for risk communication themes that emerged from this research are being used to create pre-scripted messages based on a water contamination event to be used during listening sessions with public consumers. Project outcomes will help develop risk-communication guidelines for post-incident decontamination and clearance activities following an intentional biological environmental contamination.

The EPA, in conjunction with the Pueblo City/County Health Department of Colorado, is conducting a three-year study of effective risk-communication practices during the remediation phase of a biological contamination event. The objective of this research effort is to determine the preferred mechanism of message delivery that makes it more likely that risk communications will be trusted and understood by target audiences, as well as examine risk tolerance, risk perception, and the use of social media.

Anticipating the Public's Questions during a Water Emergency

The EPA has conducted research to identify information the public will most need during a major intentional water-contamination incident. The study involved collecting information from both utility professionals and members of the public in four large metropolitan areas across the United States. The combined list of 400 questions identified during the study can be sorted into five overall question categories including (1) details about the incident and who is affected, (2) issues regarding exposure to the contaminant, (3) actions people can take to protect themselves and others, (4) acceptable uses of water and availability of alternative water supplies, and (5) response and recovery. Findings are presented in a report entitled *Need to Know: Anticipating the Public's Questions during a Water Emergency* (EPA/600/R-12/020).

Emergency Management Modernization Program (EM2P)

The Joint Project Manager-Guardian is one of the 6 Joint Project Management Offices under the Joint Program Executive Office for Chemical and Biological Defense (JPEO-CBD) is undertaking an effort to design, procure, field, train and sustain an emergency management capability for Army installations and assigned personnel. The system will provide an integrated, all-hazards Emergency Management system and enable a common operating picture, mass warning and notification, and communication with Enhanced 911.

Communicating Effectively with the Public during an Anthrax Emergency

Surveys, focus groups, and expert panels have guided the development of materials that could be used to communicate with the public during an anthrax emergency. These activities are the result of partnerships involving a host of partners, including CDC, Food and Drug Administration (FDA), EPA, Association of State and Territorial Health Officials (ASTHO), National Association of County and City Health Officials (NACCHO), National Environmental Health Association (NEHA), Association of State Drinking Water Administrators (ASDWA), and American Academy of Pediatrics (AAP), as well as state and local health agencies. CDC has used this feedback to create fact sheets, videos, social media, and web pages that aim to answer questions that members of the public would likely ask during an emergency and advise them on what they need to do to protect themselves and loved ones.

Objectives to improve communication throughout all phases of response and recovery include:

1. Enhance response communications through leveraging existing or developing new technology.
   a) Characterize the performance of existing technologies and develop innovative uses and applications that address recognized challenges in disaster communications;
   b) Develop geo-targeting technologies to support customized, response critical information dissemination based on location of recipient;
   c) Develop geo-targeting forms of communication to improve efficacy and timeliness of delivering messages to responders, the public, the media, and decision makers; and
   d) Ensure communication system interoperability.
2. Use risk communication research to develop appropriate messages and means of dissemination to all stakeholders (domestic and foreign), including decision makers, first responders, the public, and the media.

a) Conduct risk communication and risk perception research to develop public engagement campaigns that effectively address the uncertainties of public health threats;
b) Develop a fundamental understanding of what sources and forms of information are most trusted and well-received by the public, and what their expectations for information are;
c) Develop messages that incorporate findings from risk communication research, including through the use of comprehensive websites, booklets, or videos, to engage the public in educational activities related specifically to biological response and recovery pre-incident;
d) Develop message dissemination means that take into account diverse populations, including those with special needs, during an incident;
e) Develop a medical provider messaging campaign, and networks for sharing information, for patient decontamination, triage, treatment, and management; and
f) Develop methods to counteract the dissemination of erroneous information by unofficial sources.

3. Develop methods and algorithms to determine public understanding and response actions based on public messaging.
   a) Conduct basic R&D on public understanding of messaging and develop methods to assess a person's understanding of message content;

   b) Gather data to forecast and model how information is disseminated after a person receives a mobile alert;
   c) Design tabletop exercises to evaluate the effectiveness of messages and strategies to disseminate messages;
   d) Develop methods to gauge information dissemination efficacy to affected populations, including improved speed, accuracy, and overall response, due to message content and mechanism of communication; and
   e) Develop metrics to evaluate public messaging effectiveness.
4. Develop the social science approaches to understand and interpret response outcomes and amend messaging campaigns.
   a) Conduct studies to evaluate public confidence in messages and predict anticipated response to messages based on various trust levels;
   b) Identify and understand mechanisms to reduce the potential for failure in public health and safety response as a result of messaging; and
   c) Conduct studies to understand social outcomes of risk communication and messaging campaigns, including social vulnerability, response, and resilience to catastrophic biological incidents.

Goal 3: Accurately assess risk of exposure and risk of infection.

Risk assessment can be used to determine the association between the hazardous characteristics of a known infectious or potentially infectious agent or material with the activities that can result in an individual's exposure to that agent or material. Risk assessment also evaluates the likelihood that such exposure will cause an infection, the outcomes associated with an infection, and the likely impact of MCM. There is a need for more reliable information on the fate and transport of microorganisms in the multitude of environmental matrices, including food, and conditions encountered in both indoor and outdoor settings.

A solid understanding of the factors that influence the persistence and abundance of microorganisms and their dissemination, and the impact of potential mitigation methods (e.g., insecticidal treatments to prevent the redistribution of vector-borne pathogens such as Japanese encephalitis virus spread by mosquitoes or enteric bacteria spread by flies) is needed.

Scientific Program on Reaerosolization and Exposure (SPORE)

The Scientific Program on Reaerosolization and Exposure (SPORE) is an interagency collaboration between DHS S&T, DOD Defense Threat Reduction Agency (DTRA), Department of Health and Human Services (HHS) Assistant Secretary for Preparedness and Response (ASPR), CDC Anthrax Management Team, and the EPA National Homeland Security Research Center (NHSRC, which serves as the interagency lead). The purpose of the program is to understand reaerosolization to inform response decisions. Initial projects are providing empirical data on the forces required to initiate reaerosolization from selected urban surfaces, evaluation of parameters that influence reaerosolization (surface roughness, humidity, spore preparation, etc.), and comparison of surrogates (both biological and inert) to *B. anthracis*. Interagency SPORE partners are planning and reviewing future proposals among partner agencies to ensure a focused and unified research approach.

Leveraging the North American Soil Geochemical Landscapes Project (NASGLP)

Through the U.S. Geological Survey (USGS) NASGLP, over 4,800 soil samples were collected across 48 states and uniformly analyzed for more than 40 major and trace elements. EPA and USGS teamed up to expand the project to examine the presence of naturally occurring high-priority pathogens. Presence/absence data will be mapped using geographic information systems (GIS) linking location to geochemical properties of the soil, ambient meteorological conditions, soil moisture content, and land use. A graphical representation of areas within the United States that may have high probability of naturally occurring biothreat agents is critical to decision-makers in determining if a detected constituent is part of the naturally occurring environment or a contaminant associated with an accidental or intentional release.

The following objectives provide the foundation from which to build a robust, quantitative risk assessment capability to enhance response and recovery:

1. Develop approaches and algorithms to assess risk of infection from environmental exposure, including food and water, to biological agents.
   a) Generate accepted methods to establish estimates of agent infectious dose as well as critical toxic levels that correlate to a clinical outcome;
   b) Develop knowledge of exposure pathways that account for incident scenario and unique properties of the agent;
   c) Generate plant and animal models to understand and forecast clinical outcome as a function of exposure routes and concentrations; and
   d) Integrate exposure research results with existing data on industry and consumer practices into MCM selection and distribution efforts;
2. Develop reliable estimates of risk of environmental exposure for a multitude of environments, matrices, and conditions associated with wide area release scenarios.
   a) Establish key scenarios to guide fate and transport research investment, including the impact of fluids (air and water) on the spread of contaminants;

   b) Conduct research to assess microbial organism's fate, transport, and temporal natural occurrence (background soil, water, food, and aerosol levels) and geographic distribution of biological agents;
   c) Develop tools to monitor changes in agent fate and transport over spatial and temporal variation;
   d) Develop degradation algorithms to predict persistence and examine fate during mitigation and recovery procedures (e.g., food, water and wastewater distribution and collection systems);
   e) Determine the risk of exposure to residual contamination as a function of environmental conditions and types of contaminated materials/surfaces to inform recovery decisions;
   f) Evaluate the behavior of biological contaminants in fatality management operations (e.g., burial, cremation) and potential environmental release as a result of those fatality management operations; and
   g) Utilize exposure research results to develop consensus methodology to determine when areas should be repopulated.
3. Develop reliable estimates of risk to humans, animals, and plants through various exposure and transmission routes.
   a) Establish key scenarios to guide research investment on the routes of transmission for emerging and ill characterized zoonotic, non-zoonotic, and foreign plant and animal disease pathogens;
   b) Conduct research to assess transmission mechanisms; and
   c) Apply established models for contaminant distribution in water, in potential edible products, and on insects, to make quantitative estimates of risk and characterize the certainty of those risk estimates.

Goal 4: Reduce the risk of exposure and/or infection.

Methods to reduce the risk of exposure or infection are essential for rapid recovery from a catastrophic biological incident. Risk-reduction strategies include actions such as quarantine, transportation control, social distancing, evacuation, distribution of MCMs, mitigation of the spread of contamination (e.g., removing contaminated water, insecticidal treatment of vector insects, or elimination of an infected flock or herd), and decontamination. An assessment that provides quantitative estimates of risk and characterizes the certainty of those risk estimates will inform decision as to which risk-reduction strategies will be most effective. For example, current guidance on the use and application of existing decontamination methods and strategies is limited in application and may not be appropriate for all potential biological agents. Development and integration of new decontamination methods and technologies requires standardized approaches to demonstrating safety and efficacy.

Decontamination Family of Systems (DFoS)

The Joint Program Executive Office for Chemical and Biological Defense (JPEO-CBD), Joint Project Manager Protection, at the Department of Defense has established programs under the DFoS umbrella that will improve decontamination processes by developing, maturing, and fielding materiel solutions to mitigate the hazards associated with chemical, biological, and non-traditional warfare agents and radiological contamination on personnel, equipment, fixed facilities, terrain, vehicles, ships, and aircraft. Programs currently within the DFoS include: Joint Sensitive Equipment Wipe, General Purpose Decontaminants, and Contamination Indicator Decontamination Assurance System.

Advances in Decontamination for Biological Agents

The Bio-response Operational Testing and Evaluation (BOTE) Project was a multi-agency effort designed to operationally test and evaluate response to a biological incident (release of *B. anthracis* spores) from initial public health and law enforcement response through environmental remediation. The effort was led by the EPA, DHS S&T, and CDC and included participation by the DOD, the Federal Bureau of Investigations (FBI), and the Department of Energy National Laboratories. The two-phase effort was designed to operationally assess the effectiveness, efficiency, and cost implications of decontamination approaches that advanced the cleanups following the 2001 anthrax incidents or that have been developed since that time. The coordinated response, including implementation of site remediation activities, was conducted and assessed during the second phase.

The EPA's Homeland Security Research Program and the Chemical, Biological, Radiological, and Nuclear (CBRN) Consequence Management Advisory Team continue to partner to advance remediation capabilities to promote community resilience after a biological incident of significance. Products from the research efforts can be accessed at www.epa.gov/nhsrc.

Under the DHS S&T Wide Area Recovery and Resiliency Program (WARRP), the EPA and Sandia National Laboratories have partnered to develop a decontamination decision-support tool (DeconST) to aid in the assessment of remediation strategy options. DeconST incorporates a systems-thinking perspective on decontamination, considering the relationship between sampling, decontamination, and waste-management capabilities. The tool enables the use of the latest decontamination-related research and capability advances to be used to support decision making, aiding the transfer of information to decision makers. From WARRP, DeconST is being transitioned to the EPA for maintenance and further development; the tool is also to be incorporated as part of the digital dashboard tool set (TaCBoaRD) that is being developed under the DTRA's Transatlantic Collaborative Biological Resiliency Demonstration (TaCBRD).

Objectives to achieve risk reduction include:

1. Ensure effective risk reduction strategies, including decontamination, waste management, contaminant control, and reaerosolization control, for a variety of biological threats and scenarios.
    a) Generate response plan guidance, including decision support tools and methodologies, that reduces risk by accounting for scenario and agent characteristics;
    b) Conduct research to assess the impact of existing mitigation technologies and protocols;
    c) Develop technologies and guidance for mass human, animal (including household pets), and plant decontamination or destruction;

d) Conduct research on social and economic variables that promote or impede compliance capacity based on risk perception;
e) Identify consistent and efficient risk reduction methods that are readily available, inexpensive, compatible with sensitive surfaces and materials, and environmentally friendly;
f) Develop new approaches to decontamination and evaluate efficacy for new and existing decontamination approaches and procedures;
g) Develop methods to determine efficacy of risk reduction activities on the risk of exposure as a result of wide area incidents that result in a loss of property and infrastructure due to denial of use;
h) Develop outdoor (including surface waters), indoor, and water-distribution and sewagewaste-water-system risk-reduction strategies to reduce impacts and protect environmental and public health following a biological incident;
i) Develop science to support ventilation designs, including transport vehicle protective ventilation designs that provide for expedient and cost-effective isolation and negative pressure isolation rooms for use during emergencies;
j) Enhance individual survival by reducing the physical burden of personal protective equipment, integrate this capability into the responder's ensemble and use dynamic multifunctional materials that respond to threats and continually optimize between protection and burden;
k) Develop cost-effective designs to mitigate the potential occupational hazards involving airborne, vector-borne, direct contact transmission, and droplet-disseminated infectious diseases, including technologies to provide exposure protection for emergency medical professionals from airborne and surface contamination during response; and
l) Develop cost-effective and easily applied fixatives that effectively mitigate contaminant spread depending on incident scenario.

2. Develop a strong scientific basis for recommending population infection prevention measures (quarantine, isolation, and social distancing)
   a) Perform studies to ascertain the risk associated with population movements during and after multiple disasters;
   b) Develop alternative refuge options that enable access to clean air, food, and water while reducing the risk of continued exposure;

c) Develop expedient isolation methods and improved isolation capabilities to reduce exposure; and
d) Conduct systems-based analysis and develop evidence-based, optimized MCM distribution constructs, such as User-Managed Inventory (UMI), to supplement or enhance existing distribution mechanisms (e.g. stockpiles and points-of-distribution).

3. Implement risk reduction strategies to mitigate exposure from known routes of transmission, including reaerosolization
   a) Conduct research and develop technologies to mitigate transmission of emerging and ill characterized zoonotic and foreign plant and animal disease pathogens;
   b) Develop technologies to mitigate secondary reaerosolization of agents (i.e., containment of contamination) and reduce contamination spread following an initial release; and
   c) Develop protocols and implementation guidelines to reduce the transport of agents by contact with surfaces, including fomites, and by transmission from insect vectors.

Goal 5: Manage biological waste following a catastrophic incident.

A key component of the response and recovery process is the proper management of wastes generated as a result of the initial contamination incident, initial response activities, natural processes that occur in the aftermath of the incident (e.g., precipitation), and the mitigation and decontamination operations that occur in the medium- and long-term phases of the response and recovery. Waste management includes methods and protocols for reduction, treatment, and disposal of agent-contaminated waste, and must be done in coordination with the law enforcement, intelligence collection, and investigative responses. Many of the knowledge gaps in the waste management area involve uncertainties associated with application of existing well-established technologies (e.g., waste segregation, recycling, landfilling, incineration, composting) to wastes that may have trace levels of unconventional contaminants (e.g., *B. anthracis* bound in building materials). At times these unconventional wastes may be generated in exceedingly large quantities (e.g., animal carcasses from a foreign animal disease outbreak or plants from contaminated nurseries or forests). There is a need to fill knowledge gaps relating to the remediation and cleanup of water distribution systems and wastewater that may be generated as a result of cleanup activities, run-off, or other incident-specific actions. Furthermore, more needs to be known about the agent-specific behavior and environmental release of biological contaminants –including, for example, spore-forming bacteria or soil-tolerant viruses—in fatality management operations, including burial and cremation. There is also a need to develop innovative approaches to minimize contaminated waste (by, for example, vaccinating animals in an outbreak so they don't need to be euthanized) and to enhance erosion control and water treatment methods to reduce the spread of pathogens by surface-water transport.

The Human Remains Decontamination System (HRDS) family of systems

The HRDS family of systems will provide the capability to protect personnel handling and processing human remains associated with a CBRN event. The HRDS will contain CBRN-contaminated remains from the point of fatality to the Mortuary Affairs Contaminated Remains Mitigation Site, reduce the hazard/eliminate the hazard from contaminated remains, and contain remains during storage and transportation via military airlift and/or commercial aircraft. HRDS consists of three major systems: the Contaminated Human Remains Pouch, the Contaminated Human Remains Transfer Case, and the Remains Decontamination System.

I-WASTE

The EPA, with financial support from the DHS and U.S. Department of Agriculture (USDA), developed the I-WASTE Tool over the past several years. The I-WASTE Tool contains estimators for various types and volumes of waste. The tool also provides location and contact information for treatment/disposal facilities, and health and safety information to ensure public and worker safety during the removal, transport, treatment, and disposal of contaminated waste and debris.

The I-WASTE Tool is available at www2.ergweb.com/bdrtool/login.asp.

Objectives to meet waste management goals include:

1. Manage and minimize the amount of waste generated from responding to all-hazards incidents.
   a) Develop tools to manage wastes as part of an integrated response and recovery operation, including prioritization of infrastructure cleanup, waste segregation, recycling, staging, storage, treatment, transportation, disposal of wastes, and assessing the impact of decontamination decisions on waste management practices;
   b) Adapt existing waste management (e.g., treatment) technologies in a mobile deployment setting to minimize contaminant spread and to reduce transportation and disposal costs (overall waste management costs);
   c) Develop methods to determine the level of contamination present in medical waste and hospital consumables to guide disposal and/or recycle, reuse of materials; and
   d) Develop guidance for agent and scenario specific concerns regarding the handling of decontamination wastewater and wastewater arising from normally occurring activities.

2. Develop methods and criteria for selecting waste management approaches for agent-contaminated waste.
   a) Evaluate human and environmental health risks associated with use of different waste management methods to inform incident-specific decisions;
   b) Develop scientific knowledge to assess cost/benefit analysis of waste management technologies, including long-term human and environmental health impacts;
   c) Research social acceptance and develop conflict resolution processes for gaining acceptance of waste management decisions from the public;
   d) Develop knowledge and performance evaluation measures of existing waste management (e.g., treatment and disposal) technologies for known and emerging biological agents for ease of technology selection for use in an incident;
   e) Generate mitigation strategies for wastewater collection and treatment, as well as prevention of drinking water system contamination during waste management actions, to support environmental decision making for sustained operations;
   f) Develop strategies and methods to mitigate the potential release of biological agents during all waste handling operations (e.g., effective containment during operations such as removal of materials from sites, temporary storage, transport, treatment, and disposal);
   g) Develop design criteria for constructing new treatment/disposal facilities; and
   h) Develop sampling strategies for minimizing the number of environmental samples for characterizing wastes prior to transportation.
3. Develop methods and criteria for evaluating and determining appropriate disposal of contaminated human and animal remains, and infested plants.
   a) Develop scientific knowledge to compare human and environmental health risks associated with treatment and disposal methods for human and animal remains and infested plants;
   b) Develop science to support long-term environmental and human health impacts of disposal methods; and

c) Develop environmental criteria (e.g., soil type, depth to ground water, and distance to surface water) for onsite burial of animal carcasses.

Conclusion

A catastrophic biological incident would force leadership at all levels of government to make rapid, high-consequence decisions in the face of numerous uncertainties. This *Roadmap* identifies knowledge and technology gaps that currently impede the ability of relevant officials to act quickly and decisively on the basis of sound science and reliable evidence, and presents goals and objectives to speed the filling of those gaps. Although progress is already being made in these important domains, continued progress will require focused investments and coordination among Federal departments and agencies, academia, industry, and international partners as recommended in this roadmap.

APPENDIX I: DEFINITIONS

- aerosolization, n—the process of generating an aerosol; a process that generates small particles that can be carried in the air.
- biological incident, n—a natural or human-caused incident involving microbiological organisms (bacteria, fungi, and viruses) or biologically-derived toxins that pose a hazard to humans, animals, or plants (Draft Planning Guidance for Recovery Following Biological Incidents).
- biosurveillance, n—the process of gathering, integrating, interpreting, and communicating essential information related to all-hazards threats or disease activity affecting human, animal, or plant health to achieve early detection and warning, contribute to overall situational awareness of the health aspects of an incident, and to enable better decision making at all levels (The National Strategy for Biosurveillance).
- biothreat agent, n—any microorganism, virus, infectious substance, or biological product that may be engineered as a result of biotechnology, or any naturally occurring or bioengineered compo-

nent of any such microorganism, virus, infectious substance, or biological product, capable of causing: (1) death, disease or other biological malfunction in a human, an animal, a plant, or another living organism; (2) deterioration of food, water, equipment, supplies, or material of any kind; (3) or, deleterious alteration of the environment (18 USC 175).

- catastrophic biological incident, n—a natural or manmade incident, including terrorism, involving microbiological organisms (bacteria, fungi, and viruses) or biologically-derived toxins that results in extraordinary levels of mass casualties or disruption severely affecting the population, infrastructure, environment, economy, national morale and/or government functions.
- catastrophic incident, n—any natural or manmade incident, including terrorism, that results in extraordinary levels of mass casualties, damage or disruption severely affecting the population, infrastructure, environment, economy, national morale and/or government functions (NIMS).
- characterization, n—the process of obtaining specific information about a biological agent, such as its identity, genetic composition, formulation, physical properties, toxicological properties, ability to aerosolize, and persistence, and about the nature and extent of contamination of the agent, such as locations or items contaminated and the amount of contamination (Draft Planning Guidance for Recovery Following Biological Incidents).
- cleanup, n—the process of characterizing, decontaminating, and clearing a contaminated site or items, including disposal of wastes. Cleanup is a synonym for Remediation. Generally occurs after Characterization and before Clearance (Draft Planning Guidance for Recovery Following Biological Incidents).
- clearance, n—the process of determining that a cleanup goal has been met for a specific contaminant in or on a specific site or item. Generally occurs after Decontamination and before Re-occupancy (Draft Planning Guidance for Recovery Following Biological Incidents).
- community resilience, n—the ability of a network of individuals and families, businesses, governmental and nongovernmental organizations and other civic organizations to adapt to changing conditions and withstand and rapidly recover from disruption due to emergencies.

- consequence management, n—actions taken to maintain or restore essential services and manage and mitigate problems resulting from disasters and catastrophes, including natural, man-made, or terrorist incidents. Also called CM. Includes Remediation/Cleanup (i.e., Characterization, Decontamination, and Clearance) and Restoration/ Re-occupancy activities.
- contamination, n—the process of making a material or surface unclean or unsuited for its intended purpose usually by the addition or attachment of undesirable foreign substances. Used in this document to describe building, water, and outdoor exposure and external human, animal, and plant contamination.
- crisis management, n—measures to identify, acquire, and plan the use of resources needed to anticipate, prevent, and/or resolve a threat or an act of terrorism. It is predominantly a law enforcement response, normally executed under Federal law. Also called CrM. Includes Notification and First Response activities.
- critical infrastructure, n—systems, assets and networks, whether physical or virtual, so vital to the United States that the incapacity or destruction of such systems and assets would have a debilitating impact on security, national economic security, national public health or safety or any combination of those matters.
- decontamination, n—decontamination is a process that makes an item, instrument or device safe to handle and can be accomplished by cleaning with detergent and water, or cleaning in combination with disinfection or sterilization.
- emergency responder, n—includes Federal, state, local, and tribal emergency public safety, law enforcement, emergency response, emergency medical, including hospital emergency facilities, and related personnel, agencies, and authorities. See Section 2 (6), Homeland Security Act of 2002, Pub. L. 107-296, 116 Stat. 2135 (2002). Also known as Emergency Response Provider (NIMS).
- emergency response, n—the performance of actions to mitigate the consequences of an emergency for human health and safety, quality of life, the environment and property. It may also provide a basis for the resumption of normal social and economic activity.
- exposure risk, n—the probability of being exposed to an infectious agent, chemical intoxicant, or radioactive substance resulting in a degradation of health.

- evacuation, n—organized, phased, and supervised withdrawal, dispersal, or removal of civilians from dangerous or potentially dangerous areas, and their reception and care in safe areas (NIMS).
- evidence-based, adj—medicine, pertaining to the conscientious, explicit, and judicious use of current best evidence in making decisions about the care of individual patients.
- first response, n—actions taken immediately following notification of a biological incident or release. In addition to search and rescue, scene control, and law enforcement activities, first response includes initial site containment, environmental sampling and analysis, and public health activities, such as treatment of potentially exposed persons (Draft Planning Guidance for Recovery Following Biological Incidents).
- hazard, n—something that is potentially dangerous or harmful, often the root cause of an unwanted outcome; a danger or peril (NIMS).
- high consequence decision, n—a decision that could result in major disruption or has important health or economic risks. Examples of high consequence decisions in the context of this Roadmap include: ordering evacuations, quarantines, and release of MCM stockpiles.
- infection risk, n—the risk to an individual of developing an infection following exposure to a pathogenic organism (Virus, Bacteria, Fungi, etc.).
- intervention, v—to involve oneself in a situation so as to alter or hinder an action or development.
- jurisdiction, n—a range or sphere of authority. Public agencies have jurisdiction at an incident within their area of responsibility. Jurisdictional authority at an incident can be political, geographic (for example, city, county, tribal, state, or Federal boundary lines) or functional (for example, law enforcement, and public health) (NIMS).
- notification, n—the process of communicating the occurrence or potential occurrence of a biological incident through and to designated authorities who initiate First Response actions. Generally occurs as the first step in a response to a suspected or actual biological incident (Draft Planning Guidance for Recovery Following Biological Incidents).
- persistence, adj—the ability of an agent to live or endure outside of the host and remain infectious.

- reaerosolization, v—when particles collected on surfaces are re-entrained into the air stream.
- recovery, n—the development, coordination, and execution of service- and site-restoration plans; the reconstitution of government operations and services; individual, private-sector, nongovernmental, and public assistance programs to provide housing and to promote restoration; long-term care and treatment of affected persons; additional measures for social, political, environmental, and economic restoration; evaluation of the incident to identify lessons learned; post incident reporting; and development of initiatives to mitigate the effects of future incidents (NIMS).
- remediation, n—the processes of characterizing, decontaminating, and clearing a contaminated site or items, including disposal of wastes. Cleanup (Draft Planning Guidance for Recovery Following Biological Incidents).
- re-occupancy, n—the process of renovating a facility, monitoring the workers performing the renovation, and deciding when to permit re-occupation. Generally occurs after a facility has been cleared but before occupants are allowed to return (Draft Planning Guidance for Recovery Following Biological Incidents).
- response, n—activities that address the short-term, direct effects of an incident. Response includes immediate actions to save lives, protect property, and meet basic human needs. Response also includes the execution of emergency operations plans and of mitigation activities designed to limit the loss of life, personal injury, property damage, and other unfavorable outcomes. As indicated by the situation, response activities include applying intelligence and other information to lessen the effects or consequences of an incident; increased security operations; continuing investigations into nature and source of the threat; ongoing public health and agricultural surveillance and testing processes; immunizations, isolation, or quarantine; and specific law enforcement operations aimed at preempting, interdicting, or disrupting illegal activity, and apprehending actual perpetrators and bringing them to justice (NIMS).
- restoration, n—the process of renovating or refurbishing a facility; bringing it to an acceptable condition using the optimization process to determine the appropriate use and associated clearance level at which occupants may return. Generally occurs after the Clearance

Phase but before occupants are allowed to return (Draft Planning Guidance for Recovery Following Biological Incidents).

- risk, n—the probability that a substance or situation will produce harm under specified conditions. Risk is a combination of two factors: (1) the probability that an adverse event will occur (such as a specific disease or type of injury), and (2) the consequences of the adverse event (Presidential and Congressional Commission on Risk Assessment and Risk Management, 1997).
- risk assessment, n—gathering and analyzing information on what potential harm a situation poses and the likelihood that people or the environment will be harmed. [The Presidential and Congressional Commission on Risk Assessment and Risk Management, 1997] A methodological approach to estimate the potential human or environmental risk of a substance that uses hazard identification, dose–response, exposure assessment, and risk characterization.
- staying-in-place, v—the act of remaining in a designated location in order to avoid further danger elsewhere and/or to limit negative impacts in the area of the emergency. Stayingin-place is often recommended in order to facilitate the distribution of MCM or aid to individuals. This is in contrast to "shelter-in-place" which means to take immediate shelter where you are—at home, work, school, or in between.
- surge capacity, n—a system's ability to rapidly mobilize to meet an increased demand, to rapidly expand beyond normal service levels to meet the increased demand in the event of large-scale disasters or public health emergencies.
- transport, v—the movement of contaminants through environmental media (e.g., air, soil, water, groundwater).
- threat, n—an indication of possible violence, harm, or danger and may include an indication of intent and capability (NIMS).

End Notes

[1] Federal Emergency Management Agency, National Response Framework, Second Edition, Department of Homeland Security, May, 2013.

[2] Presidential Policy Directive / PPD-8: National Preparedness March 30, 2011.

[3] Subcommittee on Decontamination Standards and Technology Committee on Homeland and National Security, Draft Planning Guidance for Recovery Following Biological Incidents, National Science and Technology Council, May 2009.

[4] The following link provides the most current FDA information on drug therapy and vaccines to prepare our country for possible bioterrorism attacks: http://www.fda.gov/Drugs/EmergencyPreparedness/BioterrorismandDrugPreparedness/default.htm

INDEX

C

D

E

F

J

K

L

M

N

O

P

T

U

V

W